Life Among the Lilliputians

"On the surface, Judy DiGregorio's vignettes may seem light and simple. They are anything but. These short pieces delve into the things that really matter: the love for grandchildren, the complexities of marriage, the way we'll do anything (even carry an entire newspaper route) for our children. These essays are hilarious, touching, and often profound. This is one of those books that make you feel better about being a human being."

   --Silas House, author of *The Coal Tattoo* and *Clay's Quilt*

"Judy DiGregorio writes with a joi (e) de vivre, self-deprecating wit and a largeness of spirit that could only come from one as big-hearted, brassy and generous as she is in person. You'll love these upbeat stories and anecdotes spun from the stuff of her life and relations. I heartily endorse this book."

   --Don Williams, writer and founding editor of *New Millennium Writings*

Life Among the Lilliputians

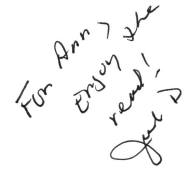

For Ann ~ the
Enjoy!
read!
Judy D

Life Among the Lilliputians

Keep on laughing!

Judy Lockhart DiGregorio

Judy L. DiGregorio

Celtic Cat Publishing

Knoxville, Tennessee

Celtic Cat Publishing
2654 Wild Fern Lane
Knoxville, Tennessee 37931
www.celticcatpublishing.com

Manufactured in the United States of America
Interior and cover design by Greyhound Books
Cover art by Jim Stovall, author of *The Writing Wright*

We look forward to hearing from you. Please send comments about this book to the publisher at the address above. For information about special educational discounts and discounts for bulk purchases, please contact Celtic Cat Publishing.

Acknowledgement: This volume includes essays and light verse previously published in *Anderson County Visions Magazine; Birmingham Arts Journal; Bless His Heart: GRITS Guide to Loving Southern Men; Bravo, Knoxville Opera Newsletter; Chicken Soup for the Beach Lovers' Soul; Chicken Soup for the Soul Christmas; EvaMag; New Millennium Writings; Literary Lunch* (anthology); *Long Story Short; Migrants and Stowaways* (anthology*); Muscadine Lines, A Southern Journal; Muscadine Lines* (anthology) and *Senior Living.*

ISBN: 9780981923802
Library of Congress Control Number: 2008937036

In memory of my mother,
Lorine Vordenbaumen Lockhart,
who opened my eyes
to the beauty of language and song.

The human race has only one effective weapon, and that is laughter.

Mark Twain

Contents

Acknowledgements

Many thanks to Dan, my first and last husband, for constant support and hours of work developing and maintaining my website; to Don Williams, writer, teacher, and friend, who helped me polish and perfect my writing; and to the Tennessee Mountain Writers, the hardest working group of writers around, for taking me under its wings and teaching me to fly.

A Boy, a Bag, a Paper Route

Several years ago, I discovered a paper route could be detrimental to a mother's health.

When our 13-year old son Chuck announced his intention of becoming a paperboy for the local paper, *The Oak Ridger*, we gave him our blessing. *The Oak Ridger* assigned him a route in the Emory Heights section of Oak Ridge, and Chuck proudly picked up his delivery bag made of green cotton fabric.

Each weekday afternoon after school, he pedaled off on his blue bicycle. He picked up his 80 papers about one-fourth mile from our house. Then he spent the next couple of hours delivering them.

It took time to learn the route and the idiosyncrasies of its customers. Some wanted their paper left on the front porch, some in the carport. Others wanted it placed beside the driveway or three inches to the left of the back step.

Collecting the monthly bill was another challenging experience. The customers who made the most money seemed to have the most excuses for not paying Chuck.

"Come back later. I only have a $100 bill."

"I'm sure I already paid you this month."

"Are you really my paperboy?"

Chuck was a dependable paperboy most of the time, even though he occasionally threw papers on the roof or into the bushes. We always knew when he had a careless day because his customers phoned us to complain. We complained, too, to Chuck.

Chuck came down with mononucleosis toward the end of his sophomore year in high school. The doctor told him to stay home for one week and rest. Chuck found a substitute paperboy for the first four days of his route. However, he couldn't find anyone to deliver the papers on Friday afternoon.

His father Dan was coaching track, and his sister Candie had dance classes. I, his faithful mother, agreed to do the route after I returned home from work. Dan promised to come and help me after track practice.

Chuck told me where to find the papers. He gave me his customer list and handed me his green *Oak Ridger* bag. I pulled the strap over my head and marched outside, ready for delivery duty.

The temperature was about 70 degrees. It was a great opportunity to be outdoors and help my son at the same time. With a smile on my face, I strolled leisurely up the block to the corner of Dayton and Carnegie.

I found several bundles of papers at the foot of a towering oak tree, just as Chuck said. I removed the *Oak Ridger* bag and untied the twine on the bundles. Then I began to stuff all 80 papers into the bag. The Friday edition included the weekend section so the papers were thicker than usual.

The bag bulged dangerously at the seams, but I forced every single paper inside. Then I tried to hoist the bag up to place the strap over my head. It was heavier than expected so I fell to my knees and tried again, resting the bag on the ground this time. The papers felt as heavy as cinder blocks.

Grabbing the tree trunk, I pulled myself up. Finally, I stood hunched over like a Neanderthal woman. The bag weighed so much that I couldn't keep my balance. How did a scrawny guy like my son have the strength to lug this huge bag of papers around and pedal a bicycle at the same time?

Lurching ahead, I pulled out my delivery list and wobbled down the road like a seasick giraffe. When I positioned the bag in front of me, I tilted forward. When I pushed the bag behind me, I leaned backward. The only way I could successfully control the bag was to perch it on my left hip and cling to it desperately as I swayed from side to side.

As I approached the first steep driveway on the route, I felt like Sisyphus pushing the rock up the mountain. For every two or three papers I delivered, I collapsed on the curb to rest. Then I had to struggle upright again. I staggered up hills and fell down driveways. I skinned both knees trying to run away from a snarling white terrier. The load of papers grew heavier instead of lighter as my legs tired.

After two hours of torture, I was not even halfway done with the route. I wondered which level of Dante's Inferno I had entered and how long it was going to last.

Suddenly a voice yelled out behind me.

"Honey, are you drunk?" asked my husband, laughing. "You're teetering all over the road."

Then he noticed the *Oak Ridger* bag swollen with papers protruding from my hip.

"Did you put all 80 papers in the bag at one time?"

"Isn't that what I was supposed to do," I snapped.

"Chuck delivers one-third of the papers at a time. Then he returns and gets another bunch. That bag must weigh a ton. No wonder you're staggering around."

"Well, I've never delivered Chuck's papers before. He didn't explain the process to me," I whined.

"Give me the bag, and I'll help you finish the route. With both of us doing it, maybe we'll be done before dark," Dan responded.

Gratefully, I relinquished the bag, and we delivered the remaining papers. Trudging home, I moaned all the way. My back ached. My neck hurt. My feet throbbed.

As I fell asleep that Friday night, I prayed fervently for Chuck's swift recovery so he could resume his paper route.

A mother will do anything for her child, but this mother will only do it once.

The Other Mary Lockhart

I'd rather be clever than dumb,
But the wit that I seek just won't come;
I think and I think
Till I feel on the brink,
But the words that pop out are 'ho hum.'

Few people get so excited that they actually forget their own name. However, at a church luncheon many years ago, I actually forgot mine.

Before I married, my last name was Lockhart. Relatives referred to my sister, Mary, and me as the Lockhart girls.Though I was older than my sister, aunts and uncles frequently mixed us up, calling me Mary and her Judy. Rather than explain who we were each time, we simply answered to either name.

My last name changed to DiGregorio when I married my husband, Dan. Then my sister married, changing her name, too, but I still thought of her as Mary Lockhart. A few years later, my brother, Walter, married a girl named Mary so now there were two Mary Lockharts in the family. To distinguish them, we referred to one as Walter's Mary and the other as Sister Mary.

I saw the two Mary's infrequently since they both lived in Texas, and Dan and I had moved to Oak Ridge,

Tennessee, where an unusual thing happened. I met a third Mary Lockhart at the church we attended, St. Stephen's Episcopal Church.

This Mary Lockhart came from Texas, like me and the other two Mary Lockharts. She had attended the same college my sister had, and her brother lived in San Antonio, the city of my birth, and the place where my parents still resided. Our children were the same ages, and Mary and I belonged to the same Mother's Day Out group. We also played volleyball and softball together on the church league teams. With so much in common, we rapidly became friends.

In addition to the three Mary Lockharts in my life, my social group included several other friends named Mary so I was constantly bombarded by the name Mary. Perhaps this partly excuses what happened next.

It was the day of the annual St. Stephen's luncheon and fashion show, an elegant affair. Dressed in our finest, we churchwomen enjoyed a delicious meal of curried chicken with rice, steamed asparagus, homemade rolls, chocolate mousse, and sherry — lots and lots of sherry, in very small glasses, of course. This was a *church* luncheon.

We ate, drank, and chatted with each other as the hours passed. As usual, I sat with my 'Mary' friends, the only non-Mary at the table. Finally, the chairwoman of the luncheon announced that it was time for the door prize, a free dinner for two at a local restaurant.

"Listen carefully, ladies. The first two women to

prove they have the same last name will win the prize."

"Mary," I whispered to my friend, Mary Lockhart, "Let's explain that my maiden name was Lockhart. It's listed on my driver's license as my middle name so that should make us eligible to win the dinner."

"It's worth a try," Mary responded. Shoving back my metal chair, I jumped to my feet, waving wildly at the chairwoman.

"Madame Chairwoman," I stated, as she acknowledged me, "Mary Lockhart and I would like to claim the prize."

"Excuse me, Judy," she replied imperiously. "How can you and Mary claim the prize? Lockhart and DiGregorio are certainly not the same last name."

"Aha," I replied confidently. "Although we do not share the same last name at present, we once did share the same last name. You see, ladies, before I married Dan DiGregorio, my maiden name was Mary Lockhart."

I had completely forgotten my name was Judy.

A stunned silence followed this remark. Then loud laughter erupted throughout the hall, especially at the table with the three Mary's.

The chairwoman looked at me sternly and declared, "Judy, you have had too many glasses of sherry. Please sit down."

As you have guessed, Mary and I won no door prize that day, but we did win many laughs. In addition, I won the nickname of 'the other Mary Lockhart,' which didn't bother me. After all, I reasoned, if I can't beat them, I might as well join them.

Life Among the Lilliputians

For most of my youth, I felt like Mrs. Gulliver living among the Lilliputians. A head taller than my friends, my older brother, and even many of my teachers, I did not appreciate my long-limbed body. I felt like a skyscraper.

Lofting me to this height was a pair of spidery legs with knobby knees and skinny ankles, accompanied by feet the size of boat oars. I longed to be dainty and petite like my girlfriends who batted their eyelashes as they looked up at a boy's face. I never looked *up* at boys. I looked *down* upon their dandruff-ridden heads.

Instead of 'gorgeous' or 'good-looking,' my nicknames included 'Wilt the Stilt,' 'Beanpole,' and 'Long Tall Sally.' Thankfully, I learned to laugh at myself early in life, and my sense of humor enabled me to deflect the insensitive comments I heard.

I'll never forget my first dance in junior high which I looked forward to with great anticipation. In preparation for the event, we practiced the mambo, the cha cha, and the jitterbug in gym class. I could float like a butterfly, but unfortunately, none of the dwarf boys at the dance invited me to flutter from my cocoon. "Cherries Pink and Apple Blossoms White" echoed from the record player as I languished on the sidelines, watching the midget boys dance with the short girls while the Amazons like me wallowed in envy and boredom.

When I lamented my height to my mother, she confessed that she, too, had dreamed of being shorter when she was a young girl. She tried to solve the problem in a unique way by asking to sleep with her sister Ellis, who at five feet, three inches tall was the shortest of Mom's five sisters. Somehow, Mother reasoned that sleeping with Ellis would magically stunt her growth. Of course, her strategy failed. Mother ended up being the tallest sister of all at five feet, nine inches.

By the age of thirteen, I had surpassed Mother's height and sprouted up like a sunflower to five feet, ten inches. My attempts to appear shorter by wearing low-heeled shoes and a flat hairdo did not succeed, though I hunched my shoulders forward and bent my knees as much as I could. During every class photo or chorus concert, I stood on the back row. If someone moved me to another row temporarily, there was an immediate outcry of 'I can't see over Judy.'

In high school, the situation improved slightly since some of the boys grew a few inches. However, I still stood out in a crowd of girls like a scarecrow in a tomato patch. My height wasn't quite the disadvantage it had been though. When I auditioned successfully for the school's modern dance group, my angular arms and legs fit in perfectly, and the judges raved over my high leaps into the air.

In college, I finally began to appreciate my height. Suddenly, being tall was an advantage, especially if you played sports. Selected for the varsity basketball team, volleyball team, and swimming team, I out jumped and out spiked my opponents, and my elongated body was a definite asset when I competed in the butterfly stroke.

My good fortune continued. Cast as Maggie, the funeral dancer, in "Brigadoon," my stature allowed me to perform dramatic arabesques and poses quite suitable to the role. Other dancing roles followed in "Kiss Me, Kate" and "Guys and Dolls." On stage, not a single person asked me 'how's the weather up there?'

At last, others viewed me as queenly and statuesque. A modeling agency hired me for part-time work, and even vertically challenged males eyed me from a different perspective. The ugly duckling had metamorphosed, maybe not into a swan but at least into a graceful ostrich. It was a great relief to leave the days behind when schoolmates laughed at my height.

Eventually, I married a good-looking Italian named Dan who was one inch shorter than I was, but my height did not bother him at all. He didn't care if I wore sneakers, flats, or three-inch stiletto heels with sexy ankle straps. Of course, I didn't often wear stiletto heels for two reasons. First, I couldn't keep my balance in them, and, secondly, Dan might get tired of talking to my chest — or maybe not.

Infrequently, I still encounter ill-bred people who can't appreciate tall women. I treat their flawed outlook with disdain since I am far above their petty views, both literally and figuratively. However, sometimes my foot accidentally sticks out and trips them.

I have traveled from stick girl to gawky teenager to mature woman. Although I am still taller than most of my friends, I no longer feel like Mrs. Gulliver. In fact, I feel quite comfortable with my height. I don't need a ladder to reach the highest shelf, and I can see over the crowd at any parade.

Yes, I have finally accepted who I am.

I am tall.

In the Bag

When I was ten years old, words spewed out of my mouth like water from a fire hose. I don't remember what I talked about, but no one was safe from my deluge, not my family, not my neighbors, not even my cat.

I chattered like a parakeet day and night whether anyone listened or not. My brother stuck his fingers in his ears whenever he saw me. My Aunt Harriet swore she would never take me to another matinee because I babbled incessantly. Even my best friend often told me to shut up.

The problem reached monumental proportions in my fifth grade class, taught by a teacher I adored, Miss Halliwell. Curly brown hair framed her thin face. She smelled of Evening in Paris perfume and wore shirtwaist dresses decorated with tiny flowers. Miss Halliwell never raised her voice and listened to her students any time we had a problem. Since I worked hard and always did my homework, Miss Halliwell and I got along well, except for my inclination to jabber too much.

Miss Halliwell did not appreciate my constant talking. If she asked a question and I knew the answer,

I blurted it out whether it was my turn or not. This made Miss Halliwell unhappy. Finally, late one spring afternoon, after she had reprimanded me several times for disturbing others, she decided to teach me a lesson.

"Judy, all year I have asked you to stop interrupting me and to stop conversing with your friends, but you seem unable to do it. Go to the back of the room and sit on the wooden stool."

The class stared as I obeyed promptly. This time Miss Halliwell meant business.

She reached into a brown filing cabinet and pulled out a large paper grocery bag.

"Perhaps this will help you keep quiet, Judy."

To my surprise, she placed the paper bag over my head. It was so big it covered my shoulders and arms, too. My skinny legs dangled in front as I perched on the stool with my hands folded on my lap, the bag resting on top of them. I tried to keep quiet, but all I could think of was how funny I must look. I began to giggle, and the bag began to shake. Soon the children sitting near me began laughing, too. Then the whole class was cackling like a flock of crows.

Miss Halliwell gave up and started smiling. Removing the paper bag, she wagged her finger at me and asked if I could be quiet the rest of the day. I promised her I could.

The next day, I struggled mightily to keep my mouth closed as I realized Miss Halliwell was out of patience with me. Thankfully, I succeeded and made it through the end of the school year without further incident.

When I recall that fifth grade year, I remember Miss Halliwell with fondness, even though she tried to curtail my talking with a paper bag. After all, better a bag on the head than a foot in the mouth.

Love on Wheels

The first time I fell in love, it was in a dark and dingy roller skating rink in El Paso.

Trapped in the gawky body of a thirteen-year old, I had no poise, no style, and no confidence. However, I did have long legs and enormous feet. One of my ancestors must have been a kangaroo.

One Saturday afternoon my parents agreed that my brother and I could go roller skating with our next door neighbor, Paula, and her brother. Since I had never visited a skating rink, I trembled with anticipation as I fastened a rubber band around my pony tail.

The magenta skirt I wore was appliquéd with black felt 45 RPM records and small musical notes. Underneath it was a multi-layered, scratchy pink crinoline given to me by my Aunt Frances on my thirteenth birthday. It puffed my skirt out so much that I looked like I was wearing a hoop skirt from "Gone with the Wind." Still, I felt almost stylish, especially wearing my black and white oxfords.

Paula's mother drove us to the rink in a 1951 canary-colored Mercury with no air conditioning. Sticky and sweating, we rolled down the car windows and let the hot Texas air blow on us. Heat waves bounced off the car hood as we scurried out into the cool, musty air of the skating rink, a welcome relief from the heat.

In the dimly lit rink, a water cooler hummed loudly as the scent of fresh popcorn wafted by from the concession stand. Skate wheels clickety-clacked across the wooden floor. Bill Haley and the Comets belted out "Rock Around the Clock." Impatient to join the action, I stood in line to rent my skates.

Naturally, the dainty white ladies' skates only went up to size nine. I was already wearing a size eleven shoe so, of course, I was forced to rent a pair of boy's skates in basic black.

Soon I forgot my embarrassment. I was too busy wind milling my arms as I strived to keep my balance on the skates. After a few spills and spins around the rink, my confidence soared and I glided on one foot, then the other. When I wanted to stop, I coasted over to the side and grabbed the rail. This was easier than using the toe brakes on the skates, which I couldn't quite master.

Paula was far more experienced than I. She dipped and twirled like a professional, skating forwards and backwards with little effort. After ten minutes in the rink, I could barely stay upright, but I already felt like an expert.

The floor teemed with teenagers of all sizes and shapes. They resembled scurrying insects, buzzing and humming with frantic energy. As I skated, I spotted a boy who looked like Elvis with slicked back hair and a pouty mouth. When I caught his eye, he winked at me. My heart stopped as my face reddened. I quickly looked away. Who was this dreamy dish? I was in love.

After Fats Domino sang "Blueberry Hill," the loudspeaker announced a ladies' choice dance. I was reluctant to participate. After all, I had barely learned to circle the rink without falling down. I had never couple skated with anyone and didn't even know how to actually do it. Which was the preferred position? Side by side holding hands or a ballroom dance position with the boy skating backwards?

When I heard Elvis croon "Love Me Tender," I knew it was a sign. I inhaled deeply as I maneuvered toward the girls and boys lining up on the side of the rink. The boy who had winked at me stood halfway down the line. I joined the line of girls skating quickly past the boys and grabbing the hand of their choice.

As I neared my intended, I flung out my left hand and smiled. Unfortunately, I couldn't slow down so I whizzed past him and the entire row of boys like a circus clown shot from a cannon. I slammed straight into the padded wall of the rink, ricocheted off, and sprawled backwards on the wooden floor. Stars circled my head as it spun from the impact.Now I understood what "falling head over heels" really meant.

With my skirt and crinoline flipped over my head, I sat stunned but unhurt. After the laughter subsided, several good-looking boys rescued me and pulled me to my feet. Some even invited me to couple skate with them. My, they were daring.

Sadly, I missed my chance with the Elvis look-alike. He skated off with a petite little blond with tiny feet who looked like Sandra Dee. I never saw him again after that afternoon at the rink.

That was the summer I learned that love does not make the world go round. Roller skates do.

The Swim to Nowhere

At eighteen, I viewed lifeguarding as the perfect summer job. I envisioned myself with a golden tan lounging around the pool surrounded by good-looking boys. I could flirt and make money for college at the same time. All I had to do was complete the certification program and apply for a summer lifeguard position.

I signed up for one of the winter quarter lifesaving classes at my university. The first night of class, I arrived at the indoor pool and changed into my one-piece black bathing suit. As I stepped onto the tiles in the humid pool area, the chlorine smell stung my nose and eyes like tear gas. Foggy pool windows dripped with condensation.

The course instructor was an intimidating fellow named Dick. Barrel-chested with slim, hairy legs, he stood about six feet, three inches tall, and weighed close to 300 pounds. Dick wore a baseball hat with the visor turned backwards as he loomed before us in faded blue swim trunks and a ragged gray sleeveless sweatshirt. He informed us that his class was the toughest lifesaving class around because he didn't want any 'sissy' lifeguards.

Leaping into the warm water like frightened minnows, we began our assigned lap swim. The pool resonated with the sound of splashing bodies gasping for air.

Over the next ten weeks, we endured a grueling training regimen fit for the Navy Seals and Sealettes. During our practice sessions, we took turns carrying a black, twenty-five pound weight to acclimate us to carrying a victim. The preferred stroke was the sidestroke with the inverted kick to prevent kneeing the victim in the back. Each of us took turns playing the victim as our classmates encircled us in their arms and dragged us around the pool, occasionally with our heads *above* the water.

We learned a variety of rescue techniques including how to approach a victim face first, how to approach one from behind, and how to approach one from underwater. We also learned defense moves to use against the victims, who often accidentally drowned their rescuers. Such a scenario had never occurred to me. Lifeguarding was potentially dangerous work!

Next, we learned the parry and thrust move. In the ten-foot section of the pool, the mock victim of the day leaped out of the water at the rescuer. The rescuer attempted to parry the leap by grabbing the victim's arm and flipping him around while securing him in a lifesaving carry. Then the rescuer carried him to the side of the pool.

Getting my arms around the chest of the massive football players was like hugging a wine barrel. Keeping them in a lifesaving carry was almost impossible, especially when the simulated victim could not float.

Only one class participant had this problem — a guy named Bill. With bones dense as lead, he sank to the bottom of the pool like a boat anchor if he did not dog paddle or tread water. When Bill was the victim of the night, we all groaned. Swimming with him in tow was like carrying a chest of drawers. Dick forced us to try anyway, even though we usually just sank to the bottom and released Bill.

Finally, the really nerve-wracking exercises began. By now, the class had shrunk to twelve students who were either too stupid or too stubborn to quit. Dick assigned us to tread water in the deep end of the pool. Then he signaled someone to sneak up behind us and catch us in a chokehold, the way an actual drowning victim might do if he or she panicked. As a safety precaution, we could pinch the attacker if they choked us too hard or if we ran out of breath underwater. I pinched hard and often.

The final class exam required that we rescue Dick through an underwater swim approach with three tries to succeed. No one rescued Dick on the first try or the second either. Although I had a massive stomachache, I managed to grab Dick on the third try and drag him to the side of the pool. Exhausted, but proud of myself, I clung to the side to catch my breath, relieved that I had passed the course.

In tremendous physical condition, I felt confident I could now help anyone who needed assistance in the water. The only problem was I no longer wanted to. My view of lifeguarding had changed significantly. It was not an idle occupation where you stood around chatting with boys and tanning your body, but a serious job where people drowned if you failed.

After all those weeks of training, I surrendered my dream of becoming a lifeguard. It wasn't the job for me. I hated the wrinkly skin and bloodshot eyes from the chlorinated water, and I was weary of being choked, pinched, and thrown around the pool. However, the final straw that affected my decision was pure vanity. I didn't look that good with wet hair.

The Consequences of Spring Fever

When the first warm breeze of spring caresses my face, an unsettling restlessness overwhelms me. I feel as wild as a young colt. I want to kick up my heels and gallop through the countryside, savoring the end of winter. One year this primeval urge catapulted me into an embarrassing situation at my university.

In the early 60's, college girls were constrained by rules of dress and behavior more rigid than corsets, though most of us did not question them. By my junior year, however, I grew tired of the double standard that allowed boys to stay out as long as they pleased while girls endured curfews — 10 p.m. on school nights, midnight on Fridays and Saturdays.

As President of the Women's Dormitory Association, I requested a meeting with the Dean of Students to discuss the inequity. He informed me the girls were locked up for their own protection, but there was no need to lock up the boys. Experience had proven that once the girls were in for the night, the boys returned to their rooms, too. Obviously, he wasn't looking out the same dorm window I was.

Night after night, after our curfew, we watched the male population wander up and down the sidewalk, many of them going to one of our favorite eating places, the A&W Root Beer Stand. It served the best root beer floats and cheeseburgers in town, accompanied by hot and crispy French fries.

One Thursday night in early spring, my roommate, Alice, and I parked ourselves at our second story open window, lamenting our female fate, and longing to join the throngs of boys still out and about after 10 p.m.

Suddenly, something snapped in me. I grabbed Alice and told her I couldn't take it any more. The night was young, and so were we. And we were hungry, too. Using the sheets from our twin beds as our escape mechanism, we could climb out the window, run down to the A&W, and return before anyone noticed. All we needed was one girl to pull up the bed sheets and drop them back down. The windows on the first floor were bolted shut so they were impassable. We couldn't return through the dorm doors because they were set to alarm after curfew.

Alice declined the adventure but agreed to handle the sheets. Only my friend, Nora, was brave enough to join me. When the coast was clear, we knotted the sheets together, tying one end to the leg of a mahogany desk, and threw them out the window. Like Spider Woman, I dangled in the air, slowly inching my way down the building. Drunk with spring fever, I felt invincible. I landed on the ground and waited for Nora. Then Alice pulled up the sheets, and we skulked down the sidewalk into the shadows, heading for the A&W about half a mile away.

Full of energy and excitement, we rushed to the A&W, gulped down our food, and sneaked back toward the dorm. Finally, Alice heard the pebbles hitting the window pane and let down the sheets. However, climbing up two stories was a lot harder than coming down. Nora leaned exhausted against the dorm after two tries. As I desperately tried to pull myself up, someone tapped me on the shoulder. It was the campus security guard dressed in his black uniform. The jig was up, and so was our short night of freedom.

For my transgression, I was forced to resign as President of the Women's Dormitory Association. Crawling out of a dorm window was not appropriate behavior for a leader of women. All three of us semi-criminals also received six weeks of social probation. We couldn't participate in any social activities and had to report to our rooms every night by 7 p.m. Though I had relished the trip to the A&W, I wasn't sure it had been worth the price.

Next year, when the first warm spring breeze tempted me to cast aside my inhibitions and common sense, I knew what I had to do. I closed the window.

—

The Shape of Things to Come

My waist has disappeared;
I don't know where it went;
But when I pass a mirror,
I see where it was sent.

Labor Day celebrates the social and economic achievements of American workers, but I recognize another kind of labor on this day — the labor of trying to squeeze a body the size of a giant potato into a swimsuit the size of a peanut. This is the labor I suffer through each summer.

Why do I punish myself by donning a swimsuit? It's simple. I have two grandsons whom I adore. Summer vacation means taking them swimming. Swimming means water. Water means suit. Suit means catastrophe.

Oh, I try to camouflage my body. I buy the stretchiest suit I can, hoping it will look loose on me. However, spandex magnifies everything. A simple roll of fat around the waist looks larger than a tractor tire.

This year, to hide my thighs, I purchased a pink cover-up skirt to match a one-piece rose suit. Unfortunately, by the time I wrapped the skirt around me, there wasn't much material left to tie it together, though I sucked in my stomach as far as I could. The skirt successfully hid my derriere, but my dimpled thighs flaunted themselves like extra large drumsticks from Kentucky Fried Chicken.

My second attempt at swimsuit fashion included trying a waist-reducing suit guaranteed to give me a figure to die for — literally. The advertisement bragged that the suit's material would improve the shape of my body while making my waist smaller. After a forty-five minute struggle, the suit and I were one, and it definitely cinched in my waist. I hurried to the pool with the grandsons to show off my new figure. Unfortunately, the suit pinched so tightly I couldn't even take a deep breath. I grew dizzy from lack of oxygen, forcing me to speak in breathy sentences a la Marilyn Monroe.

"I like your new turquoise suit," enthused a friend.

"Thank...you.... Do...I...look...thinner?

"Oh, yes."

"Great....   At...least...I'll...look...good...when...I pass...out.

The third swimsuit disaster was a two-piece number, a blue and white flowered top with matching navy skirt. The skirt sat low on my hips and didn't pinch at all. The halter top fit snugly as I fastened it around my neck. I stepped into the pool for the real test, throwing the beach ball with the grandsons. No suit problems were noted in the water. As I climbed out of the pool, I realized my halter top had rolled up and the skirt had rolled down exposing more white flesh around my middle than that found on a Beluga whale. I sank beneath the water and pulled and tugged until my various body parts were once again hidden, and I could dash to the safety of my queen-size beach towel.

I don't know why I worry about looking good in a swimsuit. Mother Nature decrees that the older we get, the harder it is to retain a youthful shape. From now on, I refuse to worry over stuffing my body into a flattering swimsuit. Instead, I'll carry a large sign with me at the pool. It will read "Wide Load."

After the summer ended, I continued my unending quest to improve my figure. I signed up for a class in Pilates, a physical fitness method developed by Joseph Pilates in the early 20th century. Many of my younger friends advocated the class and bragged how it helped tone their bodies. Of course, their bodies didn't need as much toning as mine did.

The principles of Pilates include strengthening the core muscles found in the abdominals and back. You also learn to focus your breathing while completing exercises that stretch and strengthen the body. In addition, Pilates improves balance and helps align the spine.

At the first class I met Sandy, an attractive blond instructor with more curves than a roller coaster. As she demonstrated the Pilates moves, I admired her flexibility, her grace, and her strength. When she confessed to being over 50, I was shocked. With her flat stomach, toned arms, and muscular legs, she exemplified a physically fit body. If this was what Pilates did for you, I was ready for the challenge.

The class began with floor exercises as we listened to soft drumming music in the background and stretched out on rubber mats. For the '100' exercise, we extended our legs above us with our feet in a 'V,' lifted our necks and heads like turtles, and then pressed our palms up and down 100 times as we inhaled and exhaled. Gasping for breath, I tried to imitate those around me.

Next we practiced leg circles. You extend one leg in the air and circle it clockwise for an eternity. Then, although your thigh muscles are screaming for relief, you circle the same leg counterclockwise and repeat the process on the other leg. By now my thighs were trembling so badly they were creating a breeze.

After this, Sandy demonstrated the roll-up, which is the same as a sit-up. We remained flat on the floor and raised our hands over our heads. Then we exhaled our breath as we came to a sitting position and reached for our toes. I couldn't perform even one roll-up unless I used an arm to push myself up. I bent over and reached for my toes in vain. They were so far away I could barely distinguish their rosy little toenails.

Following the roll-up was the roll-over, a pretzel-like move that forced me to roll backwards while lifting my legs over my head and attempting to touch my feet to the floor behind me. I was more successful at the next exercise, grabbing my ankles, balancing on my tailbone, and rolling backwards like a ball.

We followed up the ball move with the open-legged rocker. Sandy directed us to spread our legs wide, grab our ankles, find our balance, and then rock back and forth. Of course, I couldn't even reach my ankles. In desperation, I grabbed the backs of my thighs and hung on as I flung myself backward and then collapsed from exhaustion.

As the class progressed, I learned more Pilates moves such as planks, bridges, and push-ups. Push-ups presented a real challenge. First you stood up on your mat. Then you folded yourself forward at the waist, walking your hands out in front of you on the floor until you were stretched out in a front plank. Finally, you dropped to the mat for a push-up. I would have broken my nose if I had attempted this in the first class.

Learning to do Pilates successfully took patience and persistence, but after ten months, I finally saw some results. You can't expect miracles, however. If you start out with the body of a watermelon, don't expect to end up looking like a piece of asparagus.

My efforts in Pilates toned my body, but it still needed help. I decided that using exercise machines would burn up more calories and provide me with a more challenging workout.

Bravely, I took the plunge and enrolled at a fitness

club. My heart raced as I stared at the first monster. Slowly, I backed up. Suddenly, a man's voice yelled out, "Don't be afraid. You can do it."

With a sob in my throat, I took a deep breath and prayed for strength. Then I climbed aboard the cross-trainer. Placing my feet inside foot pads designed for a Sasquatch, I stared at the small screen on top of the machine. Which button should I push? *Fat Burn, Manual, Cardio, Quick Start*? As I clung to the rubber - tipped handlebars, a friend wandered by.

"Press *Quick Start* to get going, Judy."

"Thanks," I replied, pushing the button.

Like a sleeping Goliath, the machine jerked to life. Involuntarily, I pressed the pedals up and down, up and down. Something didn't feel quite right.

Another friend approached, observing my discomfort. "You do realize you're going backwards, don't you?" she informed me.

"Sure," I lied. "That's how I warm up."

Why couldn't I admit that I was a virginal cross trainee who knew nothing about the machine? Why was I on the machine in the first place? Because the circumference of my waist had increased from the size of a basketball to the size of Mars.

Soon I'd be forced to purchase my clothing from Penelope's Plus-Size Dress and Tent Shop with their catchy motto, "We cover your rump, no matter how big." Even more depressing was the thought of shopping at Edith's Elastic Escape Shop, for women who have lost their shape and found their fat. Goodbye, fashion.

Hello, cover-ups.

Oh, for the days when I looked like a stringbean. I ate anything I wanted with no worries, my stomach growling continuously like a motor with no 'off' button. Swimming, chasing boys, bicycling, chasing boys, playing softball, and chasing boys were but a few of my physical activities. Calories didn't stick to me because they couldn't catch me. Like a mosquito on speed, I stayed in constant motion.

When my mother taught me to make homemade fudge, pecan pralines, and angel food cakes, I devoured them as quickly as we cooked them, sometimes before anyone else in the family had more than a taste. Mom's hot, buttered yeast rolls melted in my mouth quicker than a snowfall in Florida. One morning, to my mother's horror, I sat at the breakfast table and consumed six large navel oranges, peelings and all. On days when there were no good snacks available, I gobbled up soda crackers spread with mustard. It didn't matter what I ate or how much I ate, nothing stuck to my lanky body.

Barbecue potato chips were one of my favorite foods. When I earned money babysitting, I walked to a little store down the street, purchased a large bag of chips, and then climbed to the top of an oak tree. Out of sight on the highest branch, I gobbled up each crunchy chip, lips burning from the spicy taste. Then I licked my fingers clean and returned home, not feeling the least bit guilty that I hadn't shared the bag with my three brothers and sister.

No longer can I indulge in such overeating splurges, at least, not without consequence. Now I must count the calories in each chip, cookie, or rice cake. I exercise daily to compensate for each treat I eat. Some days I'm good. Some days I'm bad.

The road ahead is long and challenging. I am no fortuneteller, but I can see my future and the shape of things to come.

It is round.

End of the Road

Taking an aerobics class does not qualify you to be an aerobics teacher any more than driving a car qualifies you to be a driving instructor. Unfortunately, I didn't understand this fact the year that I attempted to teach a friend to drive.

It was springtime in Las Vegas, New Mexico, home of New Mexico Highlands University, where my husband and I were college juniors. My father-in-law had just given us a secondhand 1958 green and white Pontiac Superchief. We were thrilled that we would no longer have to lug heavy grocery bags on foot or trudge home from classes through ice and snow. The Pontiac was a prized possession, and we treasured it. We washed and waxed it each weekend and drove it proudly around the campus.

Since we now owned a car, my friend Elsie begged me to teach her to drive. Elsie was a petite charmer who never stopped smiling. She had grown up in Houston, Texas, but her family had never owned a car. They traveled everywhere by bus or taxi. Since Elsie and her husband Bob were saving to buy their own car, Elsie wanted to surprise him by learning to drive. His birthday was approaching so this would be her special gift to him.

When I agreed to be her driving instructor, Elsie clapped her hands in delight. I had learned to drive in a small New Mexico town of 500 people that didn't even have a stoplight, but with youthful confidence I knew I could teach Elsie to drive in just a few lessons. We made plans to meet late one afternoon near the music building when the parking lot would be empty. Elsie and I spent many hours in rehearsal at the music building where we sang in the touring choir together. She had a beautiful coloratura voice that melted your heart when she sang Gershwin's "Summertime."

About 5 P.M. on the appointed day, I parked the Pontiac in the parking lot and excitedly waited for Elsie to appear. I was relieved to notice there was only one other car in the entire parking lot, a small gray Ford. It sat at the opposite end of the parking area so there was no danger of our hitting it during our practice session. Elsie exited the music building and got into the driver's side of the car as I slid over on the seat.

"I just can't wait to learn to drive, Judy."

"There's nothing to it, Elsie."

I showed her the usual things such as the gauges and the automatic gearshift. I pointed out the gas pedal and brake pedal and helped her fix the rear view mirror. Since Elsie was about a foot shorter than I was, we also adjusted the seat. I had parked the car against a concrete barrier so we needed to back it up to begin our lesson.

"Elsie, just turn the key in the ignition to the

right and move the gear shift to reverse. Look out of the rear window to make sure there's nothing behind you. Then lightly tap the gas pedal with your foot as we back up."

Tentatively, Elsie began to follow my directions. She shifted the gear to reverse and turned her head towards the rear window. Then she mashed the gas pedal down as though she were annihilating a cockroach. We barreled backwards across the parking lot like a spacecraft leaving the launch pad. The music building whizzed by in a blur. I clutched the seat screaming at Elsie to stop.

"I can't," she cried.

"Hit the brake, Elsie. Hit the brake."

"Where is it?"

Our wild ride ended with a sickening crunch and the sound of broken glass as we smashed into the Ford at the other end of the lot. The driving lesson had lasted approximately five minutes.

Elsie and I clung to each other sobbing and hysterical, unsure how our innocent birthday surprise had resulted in such a disaster. Amazingly, neither of us was hurt. However, the two automobiles suffered some moderate damage. Our beautiful green Pontiac had a huge dent in its rear fender. The Ford had a bashed - in door and broken window.

Elsie and I lived through the accident and its repercussions, our friendship intact, even if the cars weren't. The ill-fated driving lessons ended the first day they began. I resolved not to help any more friends learn to drive because sometimes a random act of kindness results in a random accident.

"*Un di felice*"

Like a mannequin on display in a Plexiglas cubicle, I hunched over a metal desk editing a technical journal. Searching diligently for stray commas and misspelled words, my eyes blurred from the strain of reading fine print. Suddenly a phone call interrupted my concentration.

"We have completed our auditions for the opera chorus of *La Traviata*, the first production of the Knoxville Opera. Only 20 singers were chosen, and you are one of them."

Stunned and grateful, I closed my eyes and clutched the phone so hard that my fingers stung. Before I could thank the caller, the monotone voice informed me how lucky I was to be a mezzo-soprano instead of a soprano.

"Why is that?" I naively asked.

"Because there was far less competition for the mezzo parts than there was for the soprano parts," the voice replied.

My ego shriveled like a piece of bacon in the microwave, but I was still thrilled to know that I would soon be appearing on stage with Mary Costa, Knoxville's very own diva.

I remembered the first time I ever heard an opera. It was in an eighth grade music class where we were forced to listen to the entire score of Verdi's *Aida*. As Amneris poured forth her frustration with Radames, I smacked my gum and wrote notes to my girlfriend, unaffected by the majesty and beauty of Verdi's melodies. Thankfully, my musical tastes matured, and I learned to appreciate all kinds of classical music, including opera.

Initially, singing with the opera chorus proved to be more tedious than exciting. We began with evening rehearsals twice a week in the University of Tennessee Music Building where we sang for hours sitting on the edge of old wooden chairs that squeaked each time we moved. Memorizing a musical score, particularly in a foreign language like Italian, required hours of practice and repetition.

Singing is a demanding physical activity. Your body is your instrument, and you must be rested to use it effectively. Otherwise, you produce some distinctly unmusical sounds, neither pleasing to the ear, nor to the audience. With a full-time job and numerous family responsibilities to fulfill, I was often tired at rehearsals. Some nights I sounded like a breathy pipe organ missing a few of its stops.

One afternoon I decided to indulge in a hot tub and sauna a few hours before the rehearsal to relieve the stress of my day and relax my voice. My strategy worked — somewhat. Not only was my throat relaxed when it was time for me to sing, but also so were my arms, my legs, and every other part of my body. In fact, I was so relaxed that I could scarcely sit or stand, and I felt as limp as a dish of freshly cooked spaghetti. My voice reflected the same lethargic state. Needless to say, I made no more visits to the hot tub or sauna before rehearsals.

After several months of long and tiring singing rehearsals, we began staging and blocking rehearsals at Knoxville's Bijou Theatre. Though a small theatre, the Bijou projected an atmosphere of Victorian elegance with its lush crimson curtains, carpeted aisles, and plush box seats. This intimate setting was an ideal place to perform because of its size and superb acoustics.

Our first evening in the Bijou, we met Mary Costa, who had the starring role of Violetta. She wore a turquoise velvet blazer that focused attention on her blue eyes and creamy complexion. Though the chorus members were in awe of Mary, she treated everyone courteously and professionally and made each of us feel comfortable on stage with her.

Finally, it was dress rehearsal week. The musical director, Ed Zambara, complained about a scene featuring the female chorus. Dressed as gypsies, we carried tambourines and struck them on the offbeat of a spirited song, "Noi Siamo Zingarelli". The song came during the party scene of Act II in the living room of Violetta's best friend, Flora, sung by Delores Zeigler. Flora's aria and our song intertwined, and we danced and sang around the loveseat where she reclined.

Since Mr. Zambara had instructed us to liven up our performance, I banged my tambourine vigorously against my hand as I performed. Then I slammed it against my side, my hip, my shoulder, and any other part of my body that I could reach, spitting out the Italian lyrics as fast as I could. Mr. Zambara encouraged the other gypsies to follow suit to liven up the scene.

By opening night, I had beaten my tambourine with such gusto and vigor that most of its silver bangles had fallen off, and the parchment covering its frame had a tear in it. As I whirled and stomped behind Flora, singing passionately from the loveseat, the thread holding the few remaining bangles snapped, showering her with metallic pieces. Flora sang on, ignoring the distraction, and I finished the number with nothing but a wooden frame in my hand.

Singing in *La Traviata* was a rewarding experience and taught me several valuable lessons. First of all, I learned that an opera requires a huge commitment of time and energy, even if you only sing in the chorus. I also learned that I was willing to pay this price just for the pleasure of singing such gorgeous music with talented professionals such as Mary Costa and Delores Zeigler. Seeing the opera come to life bit by bit on the stage thrilled me, even if I only played a small part in it.

When the opera finally ended, I missed the excitement. As I returned to my usual routine, I daydreamed at my desk. Three little words came to mind — "un di felice". Those were the words the tenor sang when he first beheld the beautiful Violetta, and those are the words I still think of when I remember performing in *La Traviata*. For me, it was truly "one happy day".

A Dog's Life Ain't So Bad

A thief lurked in the neighborhood. Rubber balls and baby dolls left outside disappeared from the yard. Muddy shoes deposited on the back porch walked away without a trace. As I stepped outside one muggy morning, I caught the culprit in action with his slobbering mouth wrapped around one of my rubber flip-flops.

Quickly I identified the dog as the black, mixed-breed mongrel that lived down the street. Each time I saw him, he slinked with his tail between his legs, never looking directly into my face, as though he had something to hide. Indeed, he often did.

Even though I loved dogs, I disliked the way this one sneaked into our yard, furtively grabbed his targeted object, and stole silently away.

I did everything I could to discourage him. Each time I saw him approach, I yelled or clapped my hands. Sometimes I even squirted him with a water gun. Nothing worked for long.

To my dismay, the dog's owners took no responsibility for his actions, no matter how I complained. After months of this aggravation, my husband, Dan, finally built a white picket fence around our yard to keep the children in and the dog out.

This solved the problem unless someone left one of the gates open by accident. The dog found other houses to pilfer and left us alone. In fact, we didn't see him for quite a long time, and I hardly remembered what he looked like. Though others continued to complain about the obnoxious dog, our yard remained undisturbed, thanks to the fence.

One warm fall evening a year or so later, Dan and I sat on the front porch watching the children ride their red tricycles. We had just eaten a fine meal of grilled steak and mashed potatoes. Dan planned to take the leftover steak in his lunch the next day.

Suddenly a stranger came to our gate and asked us if we had noticed a black, medium-sized dog in the neighborhood. The woman tearfully described how the dog had run away the week before, and she had been unable to find it. She gave us her name and phone number and begged us to call if we spotted a dog matching that description. Dan and I assured her that we would keep an eye out for the dog.

Later, as I picked up toys in the front yard, I spotted an unfamiliar dog sniffing the fence. Bedraggled and covered in mud, the black dog shied away when I tried to approach it.

"This might be the missing dog," I thought.

I sprinted into the house and grabbed the leftover steak from the refrigerator. Then I rushed outside the fence and waved it at the dog. It refused to approach until it finally smelled the steak. Then it tentatively grabbed the meat from my hand and began to hungrily devour it.

"Dan," I yelled through the screen door. "I think I've found the dog that woman was looking for. Call her and tell her to come and take a look. I'll try to keep him in our yard until she arrives."

As Dan came out to investigate, I plopped down on the ground beside the animal and timidly stroked its back as it chewed on the steak. I wanted the poor dog to feel safe and secure. Dan joined me and saw the dog feasting on the meat.

"Oh, Dan, this pitiful animal is just starving to death. Look how fast he's eating this steak."

"Good golly, are you giving my leftover steak to that dog?"

"Yes, I am. It's hungry and lost, and I feel sorry for it."

"You feel sorry for it? Do you need glasses? Don't you recognize that dog? That's the one that lives down the street that steals things from our yard. I thought we had rid ourselves of him once and for all. Now that you've fed him and petted him, he'll probably make this his permanent home."

Hastily, I stood up and took a closer look at the animal contentedly lying on the grass as he chewed up the last of the ribeye. I couldn't believe my eyes.

This was no lost dog. This was the thieving mongrel from down the street disguised under a coat of mud. Although he certainly didn't deserve it, I had just rewarded him with a steak dinner and a backrub.

A dog's life ain't so bad after all.

Of Dogs and Doors

Like a cork halfway out of a Chianti bottle, I lay wedged in the doggy door. What if someone spotted me? Even worse, what if they didn't? How did I end up in this predicament?

It was a muggy August evening when I decided to take our Siberian husky Bear for a walk after dinner and invited my husband Dan to join me. Dan wasn't interested. Neither were my children, Chuck and Candie, teenagers at the time.

"I'm not taking a key so don't lock the door," I reminded the family. Everyone assured me they had no plans to leave the house.

Walking down the deck stairs, I opened the gate to Bear's outdoor pen surrounded by an eight-foot high chain-link fence. The pen was connected by a doggy door to a small indoor pen in our garage and provided shelter from heat or bad weather. The door squeaked as Bear stuck out his head and pushed out his stocky body.

Bear and I meandered up and down the neighborhood and strolled to the creek so he could lap up some water. Finally, we returned home. I left Bear noisily slurping more water from a yellow plastic bucket and headed up the stairs to the deck. The sliding glass door was locked. So were the garage door and the front door. Both cars were gone.

Hot and tired, I longed for a cold glass of raspberry zinger tea. Since I couldn't get into the house, back to the dog pen I went. Bear sat outside on the concrete slab by his doggy door, water dripping from his mouth.

"C'mon, Bear," I said. "We're not going to waste our time. We'll take another short walk." This time we plodded slowly towards the Oak Ridge Turnpike and then returned. It was now 8:30 P.M, and the cicada chorus had begun in the back yard.

The cars were still gone. The doors remained locked. My temper climbed as high as the humidity.

"Doggone it, Bear," I groaned. "We'll take just one more trip, this time toward Emory Valley Road. Maybe we'll catch Chuck or Candie driving by, or Dan will come home."

Bear refused to make eye contact with me. His curly tail dragged behind him like a wet mop as I tugged on his leash. After another twenty minutes or so, we tramped back to the dog pen again. We were still locked out of the house.

As I took off his leash, Bear gratefully plopped on the ground. I petted him for a few minutes, staring at his doggy dog. A desperate idea sprouted in my mind.

"Bear," I declared. "I'm going to crawl into the garage through your doggy door. That way, I can open the basement door and enter the house."

A piece of musty brown carpet covered the vinyl

flap of the doggy door as added insulation against the heat and cold. Dropping on my stomach, I lifted the carpet piece and slowly pushed open the swinging door with my right arm. My head followed.

Bear's indoor pen smelled of Kibbles and Bits. An aluminum bowl half-filled with food sat in one corner. Red and white tufts of dog hair and spilled food covered the concrete floor. I grunted as I tried to force my chest through the door. The rest of my body jutted outside like a grisly latex Halloween body part.

Bear suddenly realized I had entered the territory where his food dish sat. He clamped his jaw on my ankle and began to growl.

"No, no, Bear," I begged from the other side of the doggy door. "I'm not after your food, boy."

No matter how hard I tried, I could not squeeze through the doggy door. Then I realized I couldn't move in either direction. Fleas jumped on my arm, Bear chewed on my ankle, and mosquitoes feasted on my thighs. Limp as a muslin pillowcase, I dangled in the doorway.

After I relaxed, I gave a final tug and successfully pulled myself back out of the opening. As I straightened up, I heard laughter from the neighbors who had gathered by the chain link fence to watch me. I explained my problem. One neighbor volunteered her eight-year old daughter to help me.

Within minutes, the little girl crawled through the doggy door, opened the front door of our house, and the crowd dispersed. I left Bear gobbling up his Kibbles and Bits and gratefully entered the cool house.

It was now 9:30 P.M. Dan and the children arrived shortly thereafter, professing astonishment that I had been locked out of the house. They couldn't believe I had tried to crawl through the doggy door.

"I wouldn't have tried it if I hadn't been desperate," I confessed. "The doggy door represented a window of opportunity. Unfortunately, the window was too small."

A Different Kind of Wild Turkey

I'm grateful for many things at Thanksgiving, especially for the bird. There's nothing more tantalizing than the smell of a turkey roasting in the oven. However, Thanksgiving is not the only time you can run into a turkey.

I was enjoying a hot cup of coffee and reading the afternoon paper when our grown son, Chuck, burst through the front door with a worried look on his face. He had borrowed our Honda Civic that morning to drive to work while his own car was in the shop.

"Mom, you're not going to believe this," he yelled.

My stomach cramped immediately at those words.

"I had a little accident with the Honda," Chuck continued.

"Oh, Chuck," I groaned, relieved that he wasn't hurt but annoyed that he had probably damaged our car. I followed him out the door and down the asphalt driveway. Our blue Honda Civic sat in front of the garage. It looked fine from the rear. Then Chuck pointed out the imploded windshield on the driver's side and the small dent in the roof directly above it. Grayish fuzz protruded from the splintered glass.

"Look, Mom." Chuck bent his six-foot body over and opened the car door to show me the tiny pieces of glass sparkling on the front seat. And more gray fuzz.

"What happened, Chuck? How did you drive the car home with the windshield like that?"

"I peeked in-between the broken pieces of glass to see the road."

"Well, what did you hit? What's this stuff that looks like feathers?"

"That's the part you're not going to believe. I was coming back from work. As I came to the overpass outside Oak Ridge, this huge dark object suddenly veered towards me from the right. It struck my roof and windshield with a big thud and bounced off. It scared me so bad I almost wrecked the car. I pulled right over to the side of the road."

Chuck took a breath and finished his tale. "I used my cell phone to report the accident, and the police arrived in a few minutes. I explained what happened. They saw the dented roof and cracked windshield and shook their heads."

"Looks like another one," the first officer said. "Let's take a walk down the hill to see where this thing ricocheted after it hit your car and see if we're right."

Chuck accompanied them back to the approximate point of impact. After a few minutes of combing the grass and weeds on the side of the road, they discovered the bald head and limp body of the unidentified flying object — a wild turkey gobbler that looked like he weighed about twenty pounds. The bird had an impressive wattle and a prominent tuft of bristles like a beard. He had obviously been a prime specimen.

The police informed Chuck that this was the third time that month a wild turkey had flown into someone's windshield at the same location. Why the turkeys chose that spot to fly across the highway was a mystery.

Turkeys are not renowned for their flying skills. They don't seem particularly smart either. Was it tasty berries or succulent insects that tempted them away from the safety of their usual habitat? Was it a femme fatale hen that lived in the woodlands across the road that lured them with seductive sounds? Or was it a typical male-female scenario where the gobblers decided to impress an attractive hen with a daring flight across the highway? Evidently, the gobblers didn't have enough turkey sense to realize they couldn't fly high enough or far enough to avoid the traffic.

"Son, you need to carry that turkey home for Thanksgiving," one of the officers suggested. "He'd make quite a meal. No wonder he put a dent in your roof. He was too fat to fly."

Chuck wisely decided not to bring me the bird. He feared I wouldn't use it for eating but for beating him over the head for damaging the Honda. Now we had one drivable car to share among the three of us, each of whom worked in a different location.

Later, we turned in the accident report to the insurance company.

"I've never seen Wild Turkey listed as the cause of

accident," the agent stated. "Was your son drinking?"

"No, no," we assured him. "This was the kind of wild turkey that gobbles, not the kind you guzzle." The agent chuckled as we explained the situation.

That evening I thought some more about the self-destructive behavior of the turkey gobbler. I concluded it wasn't only men who lead lives of quiet desperation.

Evidently, some turkeys do, too.

It Could Happen to Anyone

It really is a pity
When I visit a new city
That I lack the homing instincts of a pigeon.

Led blindly by my feet,
I wander down each street
But where I go, I do not know a smidgen.

No matter how well planned a trip is, unexpected problems pop up like June bugs on your porch.

On my first solo business trip to Monterey, California, I rented a small, pale blue two-door vehicle. It didn't have much leg room, and the huge dashboard pushed the steering wheel almost up against my chest. I felt as wedged in as a University of Tennessee defensive tackle in the back seat of a Volkswagen. Excited, yet nervous in the unfamiliar locale, I headed down Highway One to find my hotel.

The Monterey Peninsula is small but not small enough. I got lost several times so it took me two hours to locate the hotel. Fuchsia flowers lined the walkway to its entrance. As I headed for the registration desk, I glanced through a picture window and saw the Pacific Ocean shimmering in the distance. Even if I were stuck in boring meetings all week, at least I could enjoy my surroundings.

The weather in Monterey was too cool for air conditioning and too warm for the car heater. I preferred to drive with my windows down and inhale the fresh sea air. Since my car was fully automatic, I surveyed the buttons and levers to determine which one operated the windows. One button flipped the locks. Another opened the hood. A lever under the dash popped the trunk, but nothing affected the windows. They remained as tightly shut as a child's mouth resisting a dose of Milk of Magnesia. I finally opened the outside vent to get a breath of air.

For several days, I ignored the window problem. Then I drove into a gas station to ask for help. Since I couldn't lower my window, I opened the car door to talk to the service station attendant.

"What can I do for you, Ma'am?" he asked.

"Something's wrong with this car," I replied. "I've tried every button I've found, but the windows don't move."

"Let's see if I can help you. Why don't you hop out and let me look?"

I slid out of the car and stood beside it. The attendant sat down on the front seat and inspected the car. After a few seconds, he laughed aloud.

"What's so funny?" I asked.

"I figured out the problem," he said. "You're right about those buttons. None of them works. You need to turn this little handle here to roll down the window."

Somehow, I had overlooked a small handle protruding from an unlikely spot near the bottom of the front door.

It could happen to anyone.

❦

On another business trip to Crystal City, Va., I relished the variety of dining spots in the underground passageways that led to the Pentagon. However, I failed to appreciate the rigid rules that governed some of the establishments there, including McDonald's.

One day during lunch, I purchased a glass of orange-spiced tea and a bean sprout salad with avocado at a deli. Decked out in a business suit and heels, I traipsed up and down but couldn't find a single empty spot where I could sit and eat my lunch. Finally, I noticed that McDonald's was nearly empty so I squeezed into one of its corner tables. I had swallowed one bite when a security guard advanced on me and directed me to leave.

"Leave? Why?" I wailed.

"This area is only for McDonald's patrons, Ma'am, and that is not McDonald's food you're eating."

With that pronouncement, he grabbed my elbow and almost shoved me out the front door. I tried to look dignified as I clutched my Styrofoam food container with bean sprouts dangling from my mouth. I could see the headlines: MIDDLE-AGED WOMAN CAUGHT SNEAKING FOOD INTO MCDONALD'S.

It could happen to anyone.

❦

With several business trips under my belt, I felt like a seasoned traveler and was anxious to share my expertise with my family. On a trip to Albuquerque, N.M., with my husband Dan and daughter Candie, we rushed off the plane in Dallas, frantic to get to our next gate before the plane left us.

"We're not going to make it," my husband grumbled.

"Sure we will," I reassured him. "I'll grab the gate agent and find out where to go. Stick with me. We'll be fine."

I spotted the agent dressed in a red blazer and gray slacks and elbowed my way toward him.

"Albuquerque?" I inquired, holding up the boarding card for our flight.

He stared at me strangely and shook his head.

"No," he said, dismissing me.

"No?" I thought. "What does that mean?" I advanced on the agent again.

"Albuquerque?" I persisted, waving my boarding card in his face.

"No," he emphasized. Then he turned his back and walked away. Never had I witnessed such poor customer service.

I followed him and was about to accost him again when a woman suddenly appeared beside him. Wearing stiletto heels and skintight pants, gold jewelry sparkled on her ears, neck, and arms.

"Who's she, honey?" the blonde asked.

"I have no idea," the man replied, glaring at me, "but she's been following me all over the terminal."

Shamefacedly, I slid away as I realized that this

man was not an American Airlines agent after all. Dan and Candie had already assessed the situation and deserted me. They headed for our departure gate without my help. When I caught up with them, I tried to explain why I had harassed the unfortunate stranger. They just rolled their eyes and laughed. I didn't care what they thought.

It could happen to anyone.

The Dinkie That Wouldn't Die

B loodshot eyes greet me in the mirror. I look like the "before" advertisement for NyQuil, the cold medicine that helps you sleep. It's Dinkie's fault. She jabbered all night. I hate Dinkie.

Dinkie is a slate-gray robot about five inches tall. She has a tiny LCD face framed by yellow plastic pigtails. A friend gave her to my eight-year old grandson, Tailen. Now I know why. Dinkie never shuts up. I don't know exactly what power source operates Dinkie, but I think she is possessed.

Dinkie is clever. She walks, talks, and even snores, but she has no manners. She doesn't know when to be quiet. Like some people, Dinkie thinks the more she prattles, the more entertaining she is.

Her program menu includes several functions: clock, alarm, song, game, brushing teeth, anti-virus, and walk. The SELECT button on her back controls the functions.

Tailen enjoys the game function the most. He also enjoys hearing Dinkie talk.

"Listen to her, Grandma," Tailen squeals as he gleefully presses the buttons and shakes her up and down. "Watch how she moves!"

Dinkie's petite little form tilts from side to side when you clap your hands. Then she rhythmically shuffles along, usually off the end of our dining room table, if Tailen doesn't stop her. When she falls, Dinkie chatters louder than ever.

"Uh oh, uh oh," she bawls like a calf in distress.

When Tailen selects the song screen, Dinkie plays two eerie tunes. Both of them sound like a combination of the theme from Star Wars and the Count Dracula Suite.

Dinkie requires constant care and tending like a metallic baby. If she sneezes, she has a virus because Tailen has forgotten to brush her teeth on the toothbrush screen. He must select the anti-viral screen to kill the virus and then press the Fuel Button to refuel Dinkie. If he doesn't brush her teeth often, Dinkie gets progressively sicker. The final level of illness reveals a skull face on her LCD screen. This indicates that Dinkie is critically ill.

Unfortunately, no matter how ill she is, she won't die. She still yelps and shrieks in annoying robotic language. Dinkie's high-pitched voice penetrates pillows, blankets, and lead.

At Tailen's request, Dinkie rode with us in our Pontiac Transport on the way to Knoxville on a Sunday afternoon. She actually fell asleep for a few minutes and snored. Loudly. Everything Dinkie does is loud. Watching her sleep, I almost liked her. After all, she was a cute little tyke.

Unfortunately, Dinkie heard us talking and woke up. She screeched one of her favorite expressions — something like "I'm in the boat, I'm in the boat." After she repeated this about twenty times, I felt like screaming "I'll throw you in the moat, I'll throw you in the moat."

The first night we had her, Dinkie slept on top of a pillow in Tailen's bed. She woke him up with her midnight babbling. He didn't enjoy it, and neither did we. I stuck her beneath a large couch cushion in the living room, but that didn't stop Dinkie. Her voice pierced through the cushion and traveled right back to the bedrooms.

Finally, I buried Dinkie in the basement underneath two pillows and a blanket. That reduced the noise, but I could still faintly hear her mindless chants and incantations throughout the night.

My grandson loves Dinkie so I can't throw her away — yet. But Halloween is approaching when scary things go bump in the night and then mysteriously disappear. Maybe Dinkie will go bump in the night and disappear, too. I'll help her.

Clothes Make the Woman, Too

Fashion is in, but I am out.
Haute couture, what's that about?
When skirts are long, I trip and fall;
I've hardly any style at all.

Don't wear Prada or Cassini
Won't see me in a string bikini;
Don't be offended if this seems rude,
But my best style is clearly nude.

When I attend church services, I dress as the occasion demands. However, at one memorable service, a group of us wore outfits so bizarre they looked like advertisements for a magazine called *Vague* instead of *Vogue.*

I and other board members of Church Woman United, a racially, culturally, and theologically inclusive organization, had gathered at a small neighborhood church to celebrate World Community Day with local church women.

The autumn day turned out to be particularly cold and nasty with a chilly wind blowing. Most of us showed up for the service bundled up in winter coats with scarves, knit hats, and warm gloves. Due to the frosty weather, we wore pants instead of our usual dresses and skirts.

The wooden doors of the church creaked as we entered and heard the distant tinkle of a piano. The pastor's wife, one of our board members, welcomed us in a fashionable rust-colored woolen dress. As we removed our coats and hung them on the metal coat rack, she suddenly noticed that our entire group wore pants. Her forehead wrinkled as she looked us up and down.

"Ladies, ladies," she apologized, "I'm so sorry, but you can't come into the sanctuary dressed this way."

"What do you mean?" we questioned.

"My husband does not believe in women wearing pants in the sanctuary," she replied. "You will have to change clothes before you can participate in the service."

After this pronouncement, she turned away momentarily to respond to one of her church members tapping her on the shoulder.

In consternation, we huddled together in the vestibule. Several of us had speaking parts in the service, which began in a few minutes. No one had time to drive home and change clothes. Suddenly, the pastor's wife reappeared and motioned to us.

"Please follow me down the stairs, ladies," she asked. "I think we've found a solution to the problem."

Puzzled, we traipsed down to the church basement that smelled of perking coffee and musty clothes. Piles of tagged and sorted secondhand clothing lay in neat stacks on folding tables.

"Our annual rummage sale begins tomorrow, but I'm sure no one will mind if you borrow a skirt. Just make sure you roll up your pants so they don't show."

Giggling like naughty schoolgirls, we rushed to a table where a vast array of used skirts in varying fabrics and styles greeted us. Although there were a few skirts in good condition, most were missing buttons or had broken zippers. Frantically, we searched through the skirts, looking for long, full ones that adequately hid our trousers. We made our selections and grabbed large safety pins to secure the skirts around our waist.

Finally, our raggedy group trudged up the stairs and entered the sanctuary where the pastor prepared to begin the service. His eyes widened as we walked quickly to the pews. There were no artful mixtures of fabric, color, or style in our midst. We paraded in checkered skirts with the hem hanging out and faded corduroy skirts the color of dirt. Nothing matched what we wore on top. Our outfits ranged from ugly to uglier. With my red polka-dotted blouse and dark green cotton skirt, I resembled a large slice of watermelon with legs.

Each time one of the board members processed to the front of the church to read a scripture or lead a song, the pews shook with silent laughter. Ankle-high hosiery, previously hidden underneath pants, now displayed itself in full view a few inches below each skirt. Some errant pant legs unrolled, peeking out like children as we furtively tried to stuff them out of sight.

I have never attended a more joyful service, probably because of the snickering in the congregation. The pastor thanked us for participating and for respecting the rules of his church. After we returned the skirts to the rummage sale, we realized that clothes not only make the man. They make the woman, too.

Now Where Was I?

When I heard my daughter's words,
I thought I'd surely kill her;
I hastened to correct her;
My hair's not gray, it's silver!

Is there a connection between gray hair on the head and gray matter in the brain? Does one fade with the other? No, I firmly believe that the brain's functional capacity does not fade with one's hair color. Of course, I'm not really an expert on this because my hair's not gray. It's platinum.

In any case, I don't worry about my brain's functional capacity. I worry about its dysfunctional capacity, specifically my problem with absentmindedness.

I am not ashamed of being absentminded. As my friend Allen used to say, even the renowned theoretical physicist, Albert Einstein, might have written a grocery list that said buy protons, neutrons, and croutons.

I certainly do not compare myself to Einstein, or Frank-Einstein as my grandson, Tailen, used to call him. I am not a theoretical physicist. However, I do have a couple of theories as to what causes my absentmindedness.

Now where was I? Oh, yes, absentmindedness. If I concentrate too intensely on a task, I often block out other essential details. Unpredictable and unfavorable results often occur.

One day my mother directed me to empty a yellow plastic trash can into the burn barrel behind our house. With a book in one hand, I did as she asked, although I continued to read my novel. Unfortunately, I threw the trashcan as well as the trash into the burn barrel. I thought it was very petty for Mom to get so upset about this, but she pointed out that I had already melted two trashcans that month.

Data overload is another cause of absentmindedness. My stomach suffers gastric distress from a heavy meal such as antipasto, spaghetti with meatballs, garlic bread, and pecan praline cheesecake. My brain reacts the same way when it attempts to digest too much data. In effect, the overdose makes my brain burp. Some data inevitably leaks out. This problem occurred when I began working in the college library as a freshman.

On my first day at work, my anxiety level rose to the height of a tidal wave. I nervously listened to the head librarian's recitation of my assigned duties. Then my mind blotted out everything but the last words he uttered.

"Take the mail in the wire basket over there downstairs to so-and-so's office."

I followed his exact instructions and promptly carried off the mail — and the wire basket. Of course, I awkwardly brought the empty basket back later.

Now what was I talking about? Oh, yes, absentmindedness.

Motherhood also causes absentmindedness. There are just too many things for a mother to remember.

One morning I picked up my children from nursery school and set my purse on top of the car as I buckled their squirming bodies into their car seats. Then I drove away with the purse resting comfortably on the luggage rack. It didn't blow off because it was so full of loose change, make-up, toys, etc. People waved to me all the way home. I waved back at all the friendly people. I didn't realize they were pointing to the purse on top of my car.

Though my children are now grown, I still endure episodes of absentmindedness. Recently, I hurriedly rushed to the track after work to walk some laps. After I completed them, I discovered that I was wearing my sweatpants inside out with the garment tag waving like a flag on my rear.

The next week I visited the Fitness Club to exercise. I unpacked my tee shirt, shorts, sneakers, and socks and changed to my workout clothes. Then I headed to the abdominal bars. As I strolled, I glanced at the mirrors behind the free weights. I was shocked to see a tall woman reflected in the mirror wearing nothing but a white tee shirt and a short black slip. The poor fool had forgotten to put on her shorts. I was that fool.

With a red face, I leapt away from the mirrors and slid behind a pillar near the windows. I gazed down at my black slip in chagrin wondering how to maneuver myself unseen back to the women's dressing room. Suddenly, I realized that I was wearing black shorts beneath my slip. The slip had rolled up around my waist when I changed clothes, and I had forgotten to remove it.

Saved from complete disgrace, I reached down and jerked off the slip. Then I carefully stuffed it under the sit-up bench until I could retrieve it later. Refusing to make eye contact with anyone, I proceeded with my workout as though nothing had happened.

I proceed with my life in the same way. I ignore my bouts of absentmindedness, even though I occasionally suffer from confusion, delusion, and sometimes contusions.

After all, what can I really do about it? No one is perfect. Each of us has a weak spot, an Achilles' heel. In my case, I have an Achilles' brain.

She Had It Coming

I think that I shall never see
A bone as brittle as my knee.
It pops and snaps and locks up tight.
It aches and pains me through the night.

As stiff as any board I've seen,
My knee rules o'er me like a queen.
With humbleness, I must kowtow;
I cannot kneel so I just bow.

I am a walker. I enjoy walking as much as some people enjoy chewing gum. I have paced in empty shopping malls and congested airports. I have marched up and down office stairwells and inside smelly gymnasiums. Occasionally, I have even walked outside.

One spring morning I informed my husband Dan that I was going to walk to work. My office was less than a mile from my home if I cut through the woods behind the junior high where my husband taught eighth grade.

"Why do you want to do that?" Dan chided me. "You don't know who might be hiding in those woods."

"Come on, Dan. There's nothing in those woods but squirrels and deer, and maybe a skunk or two.

Nothing is going to attack me. If it does, I can probably outrun it anyway. It's a beautiful day. The rain has finally stopped, and I feel like getting some exercise."

I dressed for work in my favorite short-sleeved gray suit with a white blouse. Then I donned my sneakers and slung my leather purse over my left shoulder. In my right hand, I carried a pair of gray kidskin leather pumps that still smelled brand new. Smooth and shiny, they didn't have one scratch or blemish on them. I had just bought them on sale and couldn't wait to wear them.

Unlike Imelda Marcos, I didn't have thousands of shoes in every shade and style. In fact, due to my hard to fit feet, I had very few pairs of heels. Therefore, I treated those I had with great respect and tenderness. Each pair rested in its own shoebox, carefully wrapped in layers of crisp tissue paper.

With the morning sun on my face, I headed behind the school and entered the woods. I followed an uneven dirt road full of ruts, rambling through the woods without incident. Suddenly, I heard twigs snapping and branches breaking. Fearfully, I looked to my right and prepared to sprint away. Two does jumped out of the underbrush and bounded off down the road. Nothing else disturbed me for the rest of the walk. Soon I arrived at work where I proudly paraded my new heels all day.

After work, I followed the trail once more to return home. I inhaled the scent of cedar and watched the scurrying squirrels as I hiked in my sneakers, new shoes firmly clutched once more in my hand. Slowly, the day's tension left my body. Walking was much more relaxing than speeding home in the car. What had Dan been worried about?

Somehow, I took a wrong turn and ended up on a slightly different path than the one I had followed in the morning. Overhanging branches slapped me repeatedly, and mud puddles sprawled in front of me. I jumped the small ones and circled around the larger ones.

Finally, I saw the back of the junior high school in the distance. One more huge mud puddle loomed before me. Someone had thoughtfully stretched a two by four board across it.

Without a thought, I hopped up on the board placing one foot carefully in front of the other as I hummed to myself. What a perfect day.

Halfway across the plank, one end of it slipped off the muddy bank, causing me to lose my balance. I waved my arms wildly as I keeled over backwards like a redwood tree and toppled into the mud puddle. Sprawled on my back, I lay stunned for a few seconds. The sky appeared amazingly blue as I gazed at it from a horizontal position.

As my mind cleared, I realized my right arm stuck straight into the air like a flagpole. The leather pumps dangled from my hand like a prize, not a speck of mud on them. I didn't care what had happened to me. Thank heaven, I had saved the shoes.

Struggling out of the puddle, I inspected myself. My backside was completely covered in mud. I had shredded my hose and scraped my right elbow. Mud splatters dotted the front of my gray suit and my blouse. I no longer looked like a professional woman. I looked like a mud wrestler who had met her match.

As I slowly limped out of the woods, I realized I had also twisted my knee. I hoped I could make it home before Dan saw me and told me I told you so.

Unfortunately, Dan exited the side door of the junior high just as my bedraggled body staggered out of the woods. He dropped his briefcase and ran across the grass to me.

"What happened," he queried. "Are you hurt?"

"No, no, only my pride," I responded as I described my fall.

"What possessed you to walk across that plank," queried Dan. "Did you think you were a pirate or something?"

"I wasn't thinking at all," I replied. "I got so relaxed walking home that I didn't pay attention to what I was doing."

"What did you learn from this experience?" asked Dan in his sternest teacher voice.

I looked him straight in the eye.

"I learned that people who walk in the woods sometimes have accidents. If you keep lecturing me, you could have an accident, too."

That was the last time I walked to work through the woods.

Christmas Gifts and Trees

Like chocolates, Christmas gifts come in an assortment of flavors, some rich and sweet and some a little bitter.

When I remember my favorite Christmas gift as a young girl, I see a porcelain ballerina posed *en pointe* on an ivory and gold pedestal, fragile arms softly framing her heart-shaped face. Wearing a short rose and cream tutu, she gazed at me from a store window as Mother and I shopped for Christmas.

At my insistence, we entered the small, dusty store to examine her. The salesman informed us that the hand painted ballerina wore a tutu of authentic cotton lace dipped in porcelain. The hand sculpted pink flowers inset into her tutu and chestnut hair were exquisite. Such work made the figurine very expensive, but I begged my mother to buy her for Christmas, even if she were my only gift.

Each day I asked my mother whether she had purchased the ballerina. "Wait until Christmas and find out," she replied.

Finally, Christmas was just one week away, and my mother went grocery shopping, leaving me and my twelve-year old brother, Charles, to mind the three younger children. The opportunity was too tempting to miss.

Charles didn't hesitate to use his authority to boss us around while Mother was absent, but, of course, since I was a cocky eleven-year old, I ignored everything he said. To his horror, I announced my intention to find the hidden Christmas gifts and look for my ballerina.

The search began underneath my parent's double bed. Lifting up the chenille bedspread, I saw nothing but dust balls and a snoring cat. Then I peered into their bedroom closet and found only clothing and shoes. Finally, I grabbed a wooden stool and headed for the hall closet.

Behind the cotton blankets on the top shelf were several packages in brown paper bags. My heart began to race as I retrieved the bags one by one to investigate them. Charles warned me to stop and steadfastly refused to look into any of the bags himself. However, he reluctantly agreed to hold the stool while I reached for one last package on the highest shelf. Suddenly, the phone rang, and Charles ran to answer it. As the stool tipped, I lost my balance and the package in my hands hit the tile floor with a bang.

With my heart pounding, I carefully withdrew the white cardboard box inside the bag and opened it. Then I unfolded layers of white tissue paper. Nestled in the bottom of the tissue was my dream gift, the porcelain ballerina I craved so desperately, but now she was a one-armed ballerina. The other one lay beside her.

"I knew that would happen," declared my brother.

"It's your fault her arm's broken," I cried. "You shouldn't have let go of the stool when the phone rang."

Guilt, remorse, and panic overwhelmed me as I stared at the broken figurine. What had I done? Could I glue the arm back on before my mother returned?

This accident was partly *her* fault, I rationalized. She often peeked at her own Christmas gifts. Obviously, this was a genetic tendency. I had inherited her gift-peeking genes.

Mother returned from the store with a car full of grocery bags to find me weeping hysterically at the back door. I grabbed her skirt and instantly confessed my crime, begging her forgiveness.

"Oh, Judy," she cried," when your father comes home, we'll see if he can glue the arm back on, but don't you dare look at any more Christmas gifts."

Gratefully, I nodded my head as I wiped my dripping nose on my sleeve, relieved that the incident hadn't netted me worse punishment.

Somehow, my father managed to glue the arm back in place with the hairline fracture barely visible, and the Christmas gift disappeared once more from my sight.

The ballerina made her official debut on Christmas morning, much to my relief and joy. I tenderly removed her from her wrappings and gazed at the delicate beauty that had almost been destroyed by my childish impatience.

She promptly took a position of honor atop a crocheted doily on my scratched-up mahogany dresser. There she remained for many years, a vivid reminder that occasionally, at least, good things happen to bad children.

No other Christmas gift has ever made such an impression on me as the porcelain ballerina. However, some gifts I've received with minimal enthusiasm turned out to be very special gifts. One year I received such a present from my daughter, Candie — a gift certificate for a mud bath.

I hadn't enjoyed mud since I tasted my first mud pie at four years old. However, as I read the brochure accompanying the gift certificate, I became curious. The mud bath featured a special black mud from the Dead Sea that supposedly energized your body and had many beneficial qualities. I made my spa appointment and cautiously looked forward to a new experience.

On the afternoon of my visit, the spa attendant greeted me courteously. Dressed in a loose-fitting pants outfit of beige cotton, she led me past mysterious closed doors that housed other patrons participating in spa treatments. She explained the logistics of the mud bath.

I entered a dressing room and donned an old purple bathing suit I had brought with me. As I exited, the attendant wrapped my head in a soft white towel. Then she led me to a huge alabaster tub filled with blackish-gray mud.

"This mud comes directly from the Dead Sea," she proclaimed. "It's full of minerals that your body will absorb."

"So I will feel better after my mud bath?"

"Absolutely," she gushed. "This mud bath both relaxes and nourishes the body while soothing your aching muscles. The minerals in the mud cleanse impurities and will leave your skin soft as the down on a peach."

"So I will look better, too?"

"No question of it, madam," she replied.

Cautiously, I stuck one foot into the tub of mud that looked exactly like freshly poured cement. I shivered. It was cooler than I expected. Not only did the mud look like cement, but also it had the same gritty consistency.

"Just ease yourself into it," the attendant said holding my elbow.

My knees creaked as I slowly bent down. The mud smelled like crumbled leaves and damp earth as it slowly oozed over my body like quicksand. It was not a pleasant feeling. Gently, I leaned my head back against a rubber spa cushion.

New Age flute music from a nearby speaker played while soothing mint-scented fragrances from a vaporizer wafted over me. The attendant invited me to take a refreshing nap while my body soaked. I couldn't do it. If I closed my eyes, I couldn't see what might crawl out of the mud.

I began to daydream. I envisioned the Dead Sea surrounded by green and brown palm trees with feather-shaped leaves. A gentle warm breeze blew. In the shade of the arching palm trees, a group of women soaked in the mud. I imagined a conversation between two of them.

"Hannah, I missed you at the mud bath last week."

"I couldn't make it, Naomi. I had no transportation. My camel was sick. He gobbled up my good robe right off the rock where it was drying. Then he got deathly ill. It served the greedy guy right."

"Those camels will eat anything, Hannah. Mine even ate one of my sandals the other night. No wonder camel breath smells so bad."

Suddenly, the shrill ding of a bell startled me. The attendant quietly appeared like a spirit at the side of the tub. In her hand was a Polaroid camera.

"You're not taking a picture of me looking like this?" I yelped.

"We do this for all our customers," she responded. "You don't want to forget your first mud bath."

After the photo shoot, she helped me out of the thick mud which made slurping noises as I pulled out one foot, then another.

I hurried to the nearby shower, leaving muddy footprints behind me on the tile floor. Ahhh. The stinging spray of hot water felt heavenly. I scrubbed and scrubbed and scrubbed some more. The Dead Sea mud clung to me like saran wrap to cheese.

Finally, I dried off with a warm fluffy towel and dressed myself. My skin did feel softer so at least the mud bath had produced one beneficial effect. The attendant handed me the Polaroid photo. With my turbaned head sticking out, I looked like a giant turtle submerged in the mud.

I drove home feeling vaguely disappointed. I didn't feel one bit different, only dirtier. Where was the energy, the vitality I was supposed to have?

My husband looked me over when I entered the house.

"How was it?" he asked.

"Muddy," I muttered.

"I can tell," he said. "You've still got some at the top of your neck and on the back of your elbow."

The Dead Sea mud was as durable as a professional paint job. I couldn't believe how much of it remained plastered to my body for weeks after the mud bath. I went to sleep that night and dreamed I was running through the desert pursued by camels. It was easy to spot me in the dream. I was the muddy one.

When I woke up on Saturday morning, I felt surprisingly good. I couldn't wait to get out of bed. A rush of energy filled me like the Holy Spirit at Pentecost. I cleaned the house. I washed the clothes. I actually cooked a meal. I don't know if it was the Dead Sea mud or the power of suggestion. Whatever it was, I felt as charged as a new battery for days. The brochure did not lie. The mud bath did revitalize me. Candie's gift really had been a special one, even if it had been a little messy.

I haven't tried another mud bath yet, and I'm not sure I will. However, I learned one valuable thing from this adventure. If I'm ever reincarnated, I don't want to come back as a turtle.

*There's nothing like a cellular phone
To help one keep in touch;
But when I see my monthly bill,
I know I've touched too much.*

Another Christmas gift I received somewhat lukewarmly was one my husband gave me. He decided he could not make it through another year without a cell phone so he thoughtfully bought one for me, too.

I tried to appear enthusiastic, but I'm not one of those people who enjoy phone conversations. As a training specialist at a government agency for twenty-seven years, I often responded to fifty phone calls per day. The last thing I wanted to experience again was the numbing sensation of an earpiece plastered to my ear.

Although my silver cell phone was sleek and shiny as a new Corvette, it didn't turn me on. I didn't turn it on either so I received very few calls at first, except from Dan. After a month or so, I began to toy with the phone and cautiously began to build a list of contacts and phone numbers. I followed the instruction guide as best I could but with limited success.

The directions said to type in the phone number, save it, then push the letters to spell out the name. This sounded simple, but since the letters were in groups of three on the number key pad, the correct letter did not always appear on the screen. For instance, when I typed in the name of my son, Chuck, the screen read Achuck. I couldn't figure out how to delete the A so I left it. Unfortunately, most of the names that ended up in my contacts list had similar misspellings.

In the meantime, Dan gave his cell phone more attention than a new puppy. He played with it constantly, investigating every option on the menu. Then he called me to inform me of his latest discovery.

"Brring."

"Yes?"

"It's me. What are you doing?"

"I'm downstairs working on my column. What are you doing?"

"Oh, I'm upstairs playing with the phone."

One day Dan asked me for the phone number of my brother, Lester, in San Antonio. I told him to check the list of contacts on my cell phone. I knew I had input Lester's name, although I didn't know what kind of weird spelling it might have.

Dan opened my cell phone, punched the menu button, and scrolled to the list of contacts.

"What kind of gibberish is this?" he said. "These names don't make any sense. Who is Any?"

"That's my friend, Amy."

"What about cellc?"

"That's Candie's cell phone."

"Don't tell me you know someone named Faky."

"No, that was supposed to say Daly, but I couldn't make the D and L appear."

"I don't know how you recognize any of these names. Who is Frocel?"

"You know. Frolio's cell phone."

"OK, let me guess. Inha must be Inga, and Kathyc is Kathy's cell phone."

"You're catching on now."

"And Maaahele is Michelle?"

"Right."

"I still can't find your brother, Lester. Wait a minute. Is he listed as Ester?"

"Yep, I couldn't get the L to pop up."

"This is like reading hieroglyphics. Tell me who mdjjjjj is."

"Oh, that's Melissa. At least, I got the M on her name."

"I give up on the next one. It's someone called Rally."

"That's easy. Rally is Sally."

Dan shook his head as he handed the cell phone back to me, laughing.

"As long as you can decipher who those names

are, I guess it doesn't matter."

Since that day, I've added numerous other contacts to my phone, some spelled correctly and some spelled creatively. The cell phone turned out to be a valuable Christmas gift that I've grown to depend on, even if I occasionally tire of its ringing. Oops, it's ringing right now. Who can that be? Uh huh, I should have known. Just another call from Fan.

Sometimes we even get Christmas gifts after Christmas, though not necessarily a gift we want. I looked out the kitchen window one cold March morning and suddenly noticed a new tree standing in our backyard — a six foot, straggly evergreen with bits of tinsel still clinging desperately to its branches. The tree had not been there the day before. Since we had neither a son named Jack nor any magic beans, we knew one of our mischievous friends had planted the tree.

"I know exactly who did this," said my husband Dan. "It had to be Danny Sutton. That rascal loves playing practical jokes. Remember the time he took those squirt guns to that wedding?"

Dan soon confirmed that Danny was the culprit, and a new post-holiday tradition began. Each year Danny found a new spot in our yard to deposit his old Christmas tree, and it was often days later before we realized he had done it.

When he accomplished these feats, we had no idea because we never once caught him in the act. One of his most daring missions was the time he planted a decaying pine right by our front door and stuck it next to two thriving white pine trees. The tree looked so natural we didn't notice it was dead until it began to lean slightly from the rain.

Danny even managed to dump an old Christmas tree on us one June at my 50th birthday party. We celebrated at our house, and the Suttons left the party a little earlier than the other guests. A few minutes later, I escorted my friend Mary, a quiet, soft-spoken lady, to the front door to say goodnight.

As I opened the door and stepped back to let her pass, a large amorphous mass appeared from nowhere and enveloped Mary, who screeched and stumbled backwards into me. Startled by her yell, I recoiled, pushing Mary forward at the same time. Our frenzied dance continued accompanied by loud shrieks and screams until our feet accidentally tangled, and we both flopped to the floor in a heap.

Dan and the other party guests rushed over to check on us. After they realized what had attacked us, they started laughing uncontrollably. Mary and I sat brushing off pine needles from yet another wilted Christmas tree. It was six months after Christmas, but Danny Sutton had successfully struck again.

"Now we know why the Suttons had to leave the party early," said Dan as he helped us up. "Danny wanted to prop this tree in the doorway before he made his getaway. Too bad he didn't get to witness all the excitement it generated."

This year's holiday season ended months ago, and we are vigilantly watching for Danny's annual Christmas tree visit. After twenty years, the joke may finally be on him. I don't know how or when he plans to deposit his tree this year, but I do know he may be surprised when he tries it.

I can't reveal any of the details, but we have taken stringent precautions to protect our yard and house from any further Christmas tree dumping.

"Here, Brutus!"

Not Egg-zactly as Planned

As the screen door slammed shut behind me, I stepped outside into the crisp fall air and inhaled the smell of wood smoke. Down the concrete steps I skipped, heading to the chicken coop where Big Red lurked.

"Hurry and get those eggs," yelled my mother. "We've got to get to church."

I dreaded entering the dirty chicken pen so I didn't rush. I wasn't afraid to crawl through caves or hurdle down snow-covered hillsides in rusty car hoods, but I was terrified of Big Red. A cantankerous Rhode Island Red, the large cock weighed about nine pounds with a deep, broad body and a bipolar personality. He ruled over the chicken pen like Genghis Khan.

On good days, Big Red minded his own business, and gathering eggs was no problem. On bad days, he attacked two-legged invaders without warning when they dared to enter his abode. Why didn't Mama ask my brother to fetch the eggs?

Big Red's beady eyes glittered as I opened the wire gate and streaked quickly past him. I climbed the stairs into the wooden hen house that smelled of fresh straw. Peeking into each nest, I retrieved the speckled brown eggs. One black and white hen clucked angrily and pecked at me as I gently lifted her from her cozy spot to peek underneath. My chore completed, I gathered up five eggs in the folds of my full green skirt and climbed back down from the hen house. Then the trouble began.

Big Red was now in battle position, and he didn't like what he saw. For some reason, he occasionally tolerated visitors if they wore jeans or some kind of pants, but he despised skirts and dresses. Perhaps it was the rustling sound they made or the way they swished in the breeze that annoyed him. Whatever it was, the effect was similar to waving a scarlet flag at a Brahman bull.

Uneasily, I watched Big Red from the corner of my eye as I cradled the eggs in my skirt and tiptoed toward the gate. Assuming a Samurai stance, Big Red suddenly raised his wings, puffed out his chest, and pointed the claws of his right foot at me. Then he charged in full squawking voice.

"Mama, help," I cried as I attempted to run without dropping the eggs. Big Red crowed and complained loudly as we traversed the chicken yard. He was gaining on me. I could almost feel that sharp beak in my calf. The back door opened as Mama dashed out with the broom.

"Hang on, Judy," she yelled. "I'm coming." Before she reached the pen, I grabbed the eggs from my skirt.

"Get the eggs, Mama," I said, rapidly tossing them at her. Then I picked up my skirt with both hands and sprinted the last few yards to safety. Ignoring the gate, I flung myself over the wire fence and landed in the dirt, sprawling clumsily as I caught my breath.

Finally, I looked at my mother. She stood silently in her blue Sunday dress staring at the yellow egg yolks and white slime dripping down her chest. I was shocked that she hadn't caught even one egg.

"Judy," she muttered, "when Big Red chases you again, forget about the eggs. Just save yourself. That way you'll save me, too."

Alas, Big Red's disposition did not improve. One November morning he escaped from the pen and terrorized both Mama and me on the front porch. We hid behind a rocking chair until a brave neighbor heard us screaming and chased Big Red back into the chicken pen.

Mama finally tired of Big Red's antics and aggressive behavior. He met his Maker during Thanksgiving week and appeared at the holiday feast next to a bowl of dumplings. Regrettably, it wasn't a memorable meal. Big Red had the last word. He proved to be just as tough dead as he had been alive.

The Perfect Valentine's Gift

Please buy me a diamond, dear,
And I won't complain or moan-ia.
Just slip it on my finger,
And swear it's not zircon-ia.

Not every woman has the will or the capacity to sacrifice herself for her husband. Luckily for my husband, Dan, I do. When special occasions arise such as Valentine's Day, I pitch right in and help. I spend countless hours searching and shopping for a special gift Dan can give me. I usually select several gifts at the same place and then steer Dan to the store to make the final decision himself. After all, the gift is from him. He needs to take ownership. My gift-buying method saves Dan from the stress of shopping and me from the stress of not liking his gift. Could any woman do more?

I am so thoughtful that I don't demand any long-stemmed roses on Valentine's. I don't make Dan take me to dinner either. Of course, if he doesn't, he has to make me a tray of nachos because I love tostada chips topped with cheese, onions, bell peppers, and sliced jalapenos. Nachos don't do much for my breath, but they certainly help clear my sinuses.

One year just before Valentine's Day, I developed a yearning for a diamond ring. The only diamonds I possessed adorned my white gold wedding set, and my right hand needed a little sparkle, too. I decided Dan could give me a combination Valentine's Day/anniversary ring, since we celebrated our anniversary in March. I visited a local jewelry store that several friends had recommended because the owner bent over backwards to work within your budget and occasionally even negotiated the price of your purchase.

Gold and diamond jewelry twinkled under myriad display cases, but it was the display of rings that immediately caught my eye. Emeralds, rubies, and sapphires beckoned to me along with radiant diamonds.

The owner of the jewelry store greeted me as I walked by but was too busy to assist me himself so he directed an elderly woman to help me. Tastefully dressed in a simple blue wool suit, her fingers were almost hidden by large, glittering diamond rings. I gazed at them in awe as I explained that I was looking for a simple, inexpensive diamond ring. The lady was a little hard of hearing so I repeated myself several times.

"How about this," she queried, holding up a platinum anniversary band with bezel set diamonds. "It's a steal at $5000."

I gulped and shook my head, trying to convey to her that I needed something far less expensive. I was married to a teacher, not an NFL football star.

No matter what I said, the saleslady didn't hear me and reached into the display case for one spectacular diamond ring after the other. Some cost more than our house. Obviously, I was out of touch with the prices in the diamond market. Finally, I gave up, leaving the store to try my luck elsewhere.

Several days later I returned to the first jewelry store hoping to talk to the owner this time. He was busy again with another customer, and the same saleslady captured me with the same results.

The owner saw me leaving the store empty-handed for the second time and called out, "Did you find anything you liked yet?"

"No," I whispered, walking up to him. "The saleslady that's been helping me can't seem to hear anything I say. We just can't communicate."

"Mother's been having a hard time hearing lately," he answered, "but I'll be glad to assist you."

Guilt flooded over me. I had no idea the saleslady was his mother. Thankfully, the owner didn't seem offended and showed me some modest diamond rings within my price range. I found several that would be ideal gifts for Dan to give me and sent him to finalize the purchase.

The jeweler was happy to make a sale. I was happy to get a diamond ring, and Dan was happy that he had selected the perfect Valentine's Day gift for me. Behind every man, there's a woman. Behind every gift, there's a wife.

Condo Without a View

"Ocean view condo near the beach" read the brochure. I closed my eyes and visualized salty breezes, swaying palms, and warm sand between my toes. Our anniversary fell on March 16, and this year I wanted to celebrate it at the beach. When I informed my husband Dan of my idea, he groaned.

"I don't want to spend our anniversary freezing at Myrtle Beach."

"Oh, pooh. Myrtle Beach will be warm by March, and we'll get the cheap rates. Think of those juicy shrimp dinners."

We arrived at Myrtle Beach on a Saturday afternoon — the only occupants in the entire resort. Dan glared at me as we removed our luggage from the trunk. A cold rain stung our faces.

"Now take it easy, Dan. Let's just get to our room and unpack. I'm sure the weather will warm up."

"I hope so. There's no way I'm sitting on the beach when it's only 49 degrees."

We unlocked the door to our condo and confirmed that our room had an ocean view, as promised. Only you needed a telescope to see it. We had no problem seeing the Dempster Dumpster and the asphalt parking lot.

The next day Dan and I donned our bathing suits at my insistence and headed for the beach. We also wore our sweatsuits since the weather was still a little chilly. The wooden boardwalk to the ocean resembled the Great Wall of China. It went on and on over marshland and sand dunes as we stumbled along uneven boards, occasionally tripping over nails sticking up through the floor.

Finally, we arrived at the beach where a brisk wind whistled through the sand dunes. I removed my sweatsuit and made a feeble attempt to sunbathe.

"Are you crazy?" asked Dan. "You're not going to get a tan. You're going to get pneumonia."

Five minutes of goose bumps and shivering convinced me that Dan was right. I put my sweatsuit back on and suggested a short walk to warm us up. With our jackets tightly zipped and our hands stuffed into our pockets, we marched rapidly down the deserted beach. On the way back, we noticed the tide had risen and formed a shallow pool that now blocked our way. It was too cold to wade barefoot through it, but neither of us wanted to walk all the way around it. We were anxious to return to our warm condo.

"We can jump that little pool, Dan. It's not that wide. Let's give it a try."

With my lengthy legs, I sailed into the air and across the pool with no problem. I landed right on the edge of the water and barely wet my sneakers.

"Your turn, honey. Come on. You can do it."

Pumping his arms, Dan got a running start and

shot into the air like an arrow. First he went straight up. Then he came straight down. He landed with a big splash right in the middle of the pool, knee deep in icy water. His eyes bulged, his nostrils flared, and his teeth chattered, but he laughed just as loudly as I did at his misadventure. We retreated hastily to our condo before he froze completely.

The weather never improved during the week. We salvaged what we could of our vacation and anniversary celebration by visiting the malls and stuffing ourselves nightly with seafood.

"It could have been worse," I told Dan on the way back to Oak Ridge.

"How?" he responded. "It rained most of the week, and the temperature never even reached 50 degrees!"

"It's all a matter of perspective, Dan. Just think — we could have been hit by a hurricane."

February and Running Feet

If you hear the sound of running feet in February, it's not sweethearts rushing to buy Valentine's Day cards. It's not a stampede to celebrate Presidents' Day either. It's the sound of the beginning of track season.

Coaching track is quite different from coaching basketball or football. A track coach has to be as flexible as a gymnast. He has to know much more than running techniques. He also has to be familiar with the high jump, long jump, pole vault, discus, and the javelin, among other field events. Track is a multi-faceted sport, and it takes a multi-talented coach. My husband Dan worked as head track coach at a junior high school for many years. The following story comes from that experience.

Coach D., as Dan was called, was firm, yet patient with the track team, but he had high standards. He didn't allow anyone to miss track practice or to come late unless they had what he considered a valid excuse — such as death. Those who did not abide by his rules were swiftly punished, usually by running laps until they were rubber-legged and panting like the coyote who tries to catch the roadrunner.

Dan was not just a coach. He was also a mentor and motivator and prided himself on his communication skills. He interacted well with everyone, the team, the parents, and the other coaches. His favorite saying was "Do I make myself understood?"

One of Dan's many duties as a track coach was to manage and assist in running the track meets. With the numerous track and field events that occur simultaneously, many helping hands were required. Dan needed judges, timers, and starters to ensure the meets ran smoothly. Thankfully, many parents and high school track coaches always volunteered to help.

A light breeze blew one April morning as the sun shone brightly on the season's opening track meet. Parents and other spectators watched from the stands. The track area was filled with young athletes dressed in sleeveless shirts and running shorts. They were stretching and jogging to warm up as they prepared for competition.

As Dan prepared to fire the gun to start the running events, a coach from a visiting school approached him.

"Coach D., I need your help," the visiting coach said.

"Sure, Coach, what do you need?" Dan answered.

"Since you're the starter for the 100-yard dash today, I need you to remind my runner to watch the smoke when you shoot the gun. He's hearing-impaired so he won't hear it."

"No problem," replied my husband. "Which runner is it?" The coach pointed at a boy standing with a group down the track.

Dan continued shooting the starter pistol for the

other races. Then it was time to line up for the 100-yard dash. Dan walked up to the boy the coach had pointed out earlier. He lightly tapped him on the shoulder.

"I'm – Coach – D," he enunciated slowly and distinctly, using hand gestures to make his point. "Your – coach – asked – me – to – remind – you – to – watch – for – the – smoke – from – the – gun – when – the – race – starts. Just – keep – your – eyes – on – me – when – we – begin. Do – you – understand?"

The boy stared at him blankly. His mouth hung open. Dan tried again, speaking even slower and louder as he waved his hands and arms more emphatically.

"I'm – going – to – make – sure – you – know – when – the – race – starts. Just – watch – me, – O.K.?"

The boy nodded his head. Pleased that he had successfully communicated, Dan started to walk away. To his amazement, the runner suddenly yelled at him.

"OK, Coach, I'll watch for the smoke, but why can't I just listen to the gun?"

Dan had been talking to the wrong boy.

First Wife, Last Husband

After 45 years of marriage, my husband Dan still loves to introduce me as his first wife. My response is "and you're my last husband." We're both surprised we have lasted so long.

We met in English class our freshman year in college and instantly became friends. However, we didn't actually start dating until our junior year when we took Mammalian Anatomy together. Suddenly we were a couple and couldn't bear to be apart. I was shocked when Dan proposed but accepted him on the spot. Of course, like most 20-year olds, I had no idea what marriage involved.

Ours was not a lavish wedding. None of us had much money at the time. I bought my wedding dress on sale at J.C. Penney's. A knee-length cocktail dress of white chiffon, it featured spaghetti straps, tiny seed pearls on the bodice, and a full skirt. To complete the outfit, I wore a short lace jacket and a small hat covered in white roses. Dan wore a white sport coat with baggy black pants and large, horn-rimmed glasses. We laugh every time we look at our wedding photo. We look impossibly young and dorky.

After the wedding, we moved into a small, one-bedroom apartment not far from campus. Short on cash but long on love could have been our slogan. We were so poor we didn't even have a car, but we didn't care.

That spring Dan and I made a last minute decision to attend summer school. Since we had already agreed to vacate our current apartment, we were forced to search for other housing. Finally, we found a tiny house that met our requirements. It was furnished, vacant, and cheap.

The shabby wood frame house sat forlornly in a dirt yard with a small patch of grass near the front door. It was so cluttered inside with worn furniture that we had to walk single file to inspect the rooms. Besides one small bedroom, there was a bathroom, living room, and compact kitchen with a Formica table and two chairs. There were only three closets in the house. Each of them was locked. At the back of the kitchen was a windowed door with a faded green curtain. The door opened to a utility room that was also locked.

"Can we use this room for storage?" I asked.

"Sorry, it's full of my mother's stuff," explained the landlord. "So are all of those locked closets. But here's an empty wardrobe and a chest of drawers you can use."

Dan and I assumed the landlord's mother had recently died, and he hadn't yet cleaned out the house. However, we were too polite to ask.

We didn't really like the house, but decided we could endure it for the six-week summer term. The rent was incredibly low, and the landlord agreed to pay for utilities. In addition, if anything broke, the landlord was readily available since he lived directly behind us.

We carried our suitcases and boxes into the stuffy house and settled down for the night in the creaky double bed. I had an uneasy feeling.

"Dan, I feel like someone's watching us."

"How could anyone be watching us? This house is so little there's barely room for us," Dan scoffed.

"Maybe a ghost lives in here," I responded.

Most of the light fixtures in the house had no light bulbs. Those that did had only 60-watt bulbs. The dim lighting created a spooky atmosphere. The next day, we bought several packages of 100-watt light bulbs to help brighten up the place.

No matter how many bulbs we replaced, the new bulbs disappeared and were replaced by the dim ones. When we returned home, the house was once more dark and dreary looking. Puzzled, we questioned the landlord, but he professed ignorance.

Other strange events occurred. Sometimes we smelled fresh coffee, although we hadn't brewed any. Occasionally, we heard voices murmuring, even though we were the only ones in the house.

One afternoon, after living in the house almost a week, we returned from classes earlier than usual. As we entered the front door, we smelled pinto beans cooking and heard a pot bang against the stove. We tiptoed through the house and peeped through the kitchen door. In front of us stood an elderly woman about five feet tall in a shapeless black dress and black hose. Startled to see us, she shrieked, waved her arms, and ran towards the utility room that was now unlocked. Cautiously, we followed her. In the utility room we saw a twin bed, a chest of drawers, and a nightstand. The stranger, muttering and mumbling, fled through a door at the back of the utility room. To our surprise, she headed straight for our landlord's house.

"Who is that, Dan?" I asked.

"I don't know, but we're going to find out," Dan answered, as we followed the fugitive.

The landlord answered our questions with an ingratiating smile.

"Oh, don't worry," he placated us. "That woman's my mother. Didn't I tell you she lives with you? She shares the kitchen and sleeps in the utility room."

Dan and I were shocked to hear this. We informed our landlord that three was a crowd, no matter how cheap the rent was. Hastily packing up our meager belongings, we left the house. Luckily, the landlord agreed to refund us part of the rent.

We then located a one-bedroom apartment a few blocks from the campus that was unexpectedly vacant. We did a quick walk-through and paid the rent on the spot to hold the apartment.

This apartment was a step up from the squalid little house. It had a large living room for entertaining, a spacious bedroom, and plenty of closets. Not one of them was locked. We arranged to move in that afternoon. After we unpacked our cardboard boxes, we examined the apartment a little closer. Then we discovered why the apartment was such a bargain. The bathroom was about 100 yards away, attached to the back of another building. We had to share it with several other tenants.

Dan and I were disgusted with ourselves at our naiveté. Within one short week, we had made two poor decisions. We were still long on love and short on cash. For the rest of that summer, we were also short of a bathroom.

By now we had been married several months, and the honeymoon period was beginning to expire. Reality set in. Dan came from a traditional Italian family and expected me to handle all the housekeeping chores. I attended school full-time and held an undergraduate assistantship so I had many demands on my time. Housekeeping was not a priority.

It took quite a while for us to iron out differences of opinion as to who should do what when. When I became frustrated with Dan, I always followed the same routine. I stomped to the bedroom, packed my striped brown suitcase, and marched out the front door, slamming it behind me. The problem was I couldn't go very far without a car. The suitcase was heavy. I usually walked around the block a few times until I made my point. Then I returned home until the next argument. The neighbors knew the state of our marital affairs as soon as they saw me walk by with my suitcase.

Getting married was easy. Staying married year after year was hard. Although we enjoyed each other's company, sometimes we just got tired of each other. One memorable day Dan criticized me for taking too long at the grocery store while he was babysitting our young children, Chuck and Candie. I got so angry that I threw a bag of pinto beans at him. Of course, he ducked. The bag hit the wall and split open, scattering beans everywhere. We picked them up for months.

Eventually, Dan became a physical science teacher and head football coach at the local junior high school. Our son Chuck played on the team, and our daughter Candie was a cheerleader. A loyal fan, of course, I rode the noisy pep bus with the rowdy junior high students to every single game including those played in Crossville, Lafollette, Chattanooga, Jacksboro, and Clinton. Football was definitely a family affair at our house.

For the banquet that evening, I dressed to match the school colors of blue and gold. I wore a two-piece blue suit with a yellow scarf around my neck. Someone pinned a lovely chrysanthemum corsage on my jacket as an added bonus. Feeling festive and elegant, I joined my husband and the others from the head table and progressed through the food line in the cafeteria. Without qualm I filled my plate with samples of homemade casseroles, fried chicken, tossed salads, and chocolate meringue pie. Then I sat down by Dan at the head table that was cheerfully decorated with potted mums and blue and gold streamers.

After we ate, Dan pushed back his chair and quieted down the crowd. Then he introduced me and thanked me for my support. As I stood up, a girl at the table nearby pointed at me and giggled. Confident she was admiring my outfit, I smiled broadly at her and resumed my seat. Dan spoke about the winning season and the sacrifices the football players and their families had made. Then he introduced the speaker and other guests and finally presented the team awards.

After the banquet, many parents and students came to the head table to shake Dan's hand and thank him for his hard work. However, when they looked at me, many people snickered. I wondered if I had lipstick on my teeth and ran my tongue over them quickly.

The long evening finally ended, and Dan, Chuck, Candie, and I arrived home about 10 p.m. The teenagers ignored us as usual and went to bed. I changed into my pajamas and prepared to clean my face. Then I looked into the bathroom mirror. A shocking sight greeted me. On the lower right-hand side of my chin sat a large cucumber seed. Evidently, it had stuck to me when I ate my salad. Now I understood the strange looks and snickers at the banquet.

"Dan," I wailed, "why didn't you mention the cucumber seed on my chin?"

"Cucumber seed?" he replied as he stared at me. "I thought it was a wart."

Obviously, the longer a man is married, the less attention he pays to his wife's appearance.

Over the years, we have grown calmer, wiser and

grayer. We've been married so long that Dan's stories have become my stories, and mine have become his. We can't remember who actually told them in the first place. A relationship comfortable as an old pair of shoes has replaced the bloom of young love. We have learned to respect each other and appreciate our differences. Dan will never enjoy musicals as much as I do. I will never like football as much as he does. It doesn't matter. We still love each other.

Staying married for 45 years takes commitment, perseverance, and a sense of humor. We couldn't have made it without following the advice of Franklin D. Roosevelt who said "When you get to the end of your rope, tie a knot and hang on." Dan and I are still hanging on.

Make Love, Not Sausage

New relationships must be as carefully handled as spumoni ice cream on a hot summer day. Otherwise, they can easily melt away.

When my husband Dan brought me home for the first time to meet his family, many years ago, I resolved to impress them with my even temperament and sparkling personality. They would immediately understand why their son had chosen me as his future bride.

Dan's father inclined his head of thick black hair as he shook my hand. He had huge muscular arms from his years in the coal mines. Dan's mother wore her gray hair pulled back in a bun. Her smoldering green eyes stared intensely at me.

"*Piacere* (my pleasure)," she said, hugging me to her.

Dan's parents were a bit nervous, just like me, but I knew they wanted to make me feel welcome. They decided to do it by honoring me in a traditional Italian manner — by preparing and serving a meal with homemade sausage.

I'm a pastry lover, not a meat lover. I would have preferred homemade *canolli* or *biscotti*, but I didn't want to offend Dan's family by telling them that.

To show what a special guest I was, they invited me to help make the sausage. Soon I stood in the blue and white kitchen with a muslin apron wrapped around me. I admired the copper pots and pans hanging on one wall as I inhaled the smell of fresh garlic and percolating coffee.

To my horror, Dan's mother directed me to stand at the sink and help wash fresh lamb intestines. I had no idea these were used to make sausage. The slippery, slimy gelatinous mass of intestines repulsed me. The kitchen looked like a scene from a horror movie with intestines flung everywhere — the table, the countertops, and the floor. They looked like primeval monsters struggling to evolve into a higher life form. I expected them to start crawling towards me at any minute. One of them had a dark spot resembling an eye. I felt it watching me.

We stood at the sink as we ran water through each intestine until it was perfectly clean, and the water ran clear. Then we plopped the intestines into huge pots of boiling water. The stench was sickening. It smelled like a combination of road kill and camel dung. After the intestines were sterilized by boiling, we stretched them out like tentacles on the table and counter tops to cool them.

Next we ground up the lamb meat. We added black pepper, red pepper, chopped garlic, and salt. We poked the meat mixture down into the cooled intestines through a metal funnel. First we tied the bottom of the intestine with a piece of string. Then we inserted the funnel into the top, using our fingers or a metal spoon to force the meat to the bottom of the intestine. When the intestine was full, we tied off the top with another piece of string. It was a tedious and messy process. I hated doing it, but I kept a ghastly smile plastered on my sweaty face.

Finally, we fried the sausages in hot oil on a gas stove until every piece of sausage was crisp. My future in-laws were pleased at my efforts. They patted my back and repeatedly pinched my cheek murmuring *bella, bella*.

I looked properly grateful for the opportunity to learn to make homemade sausage. Finally, we finished frying all of them. I relaxed.

Suddenly, I remembered that I was expected to eat the sausages, too. Waves of nausea swept over me at the thought. At least I had several hours before the evening meal.

The smell of simmering tomato sauce soon replaced the greasy odor of the fried sausages as Dan's mother continued preparations for dinner.

That evening we sat down for supper and consumed platefuls of spaghetti cooked *al dente*, with just the right amount of chewiness. Fragrant sauce spiced with red wine, celery, garlic, and oregano covered the pasta. Hand grated Parmesan and Romano cheese topped each serving. Homemade red wine from zinfandel grapes filled our glasses. I began to forget the sausages.

Then Dan's mother left the table and returned with a huge platter of sausages. Dan's father passed a stack of crusty Italian bread.

"*Mangia, mangia* (eat, eat)," they encouraged me, offering me the bread and sausage.

In desperation, I stabbed a small sausage and wrapped it in a slice of bread. I took a teeny bite off the top as though I were eating toxic waste.

"You like?" asked Dan's mother.

"Um hum," I mumbled, gagging.

I continued to nibble on the bread while slowly squeezing the sausage out of the bottom of the sandwich. In my lap lay a large white paper napkin that became the repository for the sausage. I munched on until I had completely devoured the piece of bread, thinking that at last my ordeal was over. It wasn't.

"Judy, eat some more. Take another one," begged Dan's father.

Despite my protests and increasingly violent hand gestures, another sausage landed on my plate. We went through this same routine again and again until I felt as stuffed as the sausages. My napkin was now swollen with a pile of meaty monsters. I had no idea how to gracefully discard them.

Luckily, my future mother-in-law excused herself to answer the phone. Dan's father left the table to get more wine. I leapt from my chair holding the ends of my napkin tightly together. Dan shook his finger at me.

"I know what you've been up to," he whispered.

"If you tell on me, I'll force every one of these sausages down your throat," I muttered as I fled, pretending to have a coughing fit. I hid the sausages under the bed.

Later that night, I sneaked to the back yard and fed the sausages to the family dog, a black cocker spaniel. He looked at me with adoring eyes. At least I had impressed him, if no one else.

When our visit with Dan's family ended, I felt satisfied. Our relationship was off to a good start. I liked them. They liked me. They had honored me by making the meal of homemade sausage. I had honored them by eating it. I just hoped next time they served tiramisu.

About the Author

Judy Lockhart DiGregorio is an Army brat from San Antonio, Texas, who resides in Oak Ridge, TN. Her work is included in numerous anthologies and a wide variety of publications including the Army-Navy Times, The Writer, ByLine Magazine, and the Chicken Soup books. Judy is a YWCA Woman of Distinction in the Arts. In her spare time Judy volunteers with the Oak Ridge Chamber of Commerce, gives concerts of Hispanic music, and does community theatre at the Oak Ridge Playhouse. The Tennessee Arts Commission nominated Judy to their online artist registry for outstanding southern artists, www.southernartistry. org/ in 2006.

Visit Judy's website and blog at http://judyjabber. com.

About Celtic Cat Publishing

Celtic Cat Publishing was founded in 1995 to publish emerging and established writers.

The following works are available from Celtic Cat Publishing at www.celticcatpublishing.com, from Amazon.com and from major bookstores.

Exile: Poems of an Irish Immigrant by James B. Johnston ($9.95)

Marginal Notes by Frank Jamison ($12.00)

Rough Ascension and Other Poems of Science by Arthur J. Stewart ($15.00)

Bushido: The Virtues of Rei and Makoto by Arthur J. Stewart ($15.00)

Gathering Stones by KB Ballentine ($15.00)

Ebbing & Flowing Springs: New and Selected Poems and Prose (1976-2001) by Jeff Daniel Marion ($25.00)

My Barbie Was an Amputee by Angie Vicars ($15.00)

One for Each Night: Chanukah Tales and Recipes by Marilyn Kallet ($15.00)

LaVergne, TN USA
24 May 2010
183685LV00002B/4/P